MORAVIA MAGNA

MORAVIA MAGNA

THE GREAT MORAVIAN EMPIRE

Its Art and Times

JÁN DEKAN

Photographs
ALEXANDER PAUL, Sr.
and
ALEXANDER PAUL, Jr.

CONTROL DATA ARTS
Minneapolis, Minnesota
1981

MORAVIA MAGNA: The Great Moravian Empire by Ján Dekan
Photographs by Alexander Paul, Sr. and Alexander Paul, Jr.
English translation by Heather Trebatická
Technical information in the catalog by Dr. Mária Rejholcová
Editor: Emília Kučerová
Designer: Ivan J. Kovačevič

First edited and adapted English Language Edition
Editor: Ann M. Waters
Supervising editor: Pamela Espeland

Library of Congress Cataloging in Publication Data

Dekan, Ján.
Moravia Magna: The Great Moravian Empire.
Based on: Veľká Morava / Ján Dekan. — Bratislava, Czechoslovakia: Tatran, 1976.
Bibliography: p.
1. Moravia (Czechoslovakia) — History. I. Title.
DB2386.D44   943.7'2   81-2119
ISBN   0-89893-084-7   AACR2

CONTENTS

THE GREAT MORAVIAN EMPIRE: ITS ART AND TIMES

The Art of the Pontic Steppe

Only fragments remain of what was once the Great Moravian Empire, but they speak of a culture that flourished long ago. In a land bounded by four rivers — the Danube, the Morava, the Elbe, and the Tisza — that covers part of present-day Czechoslovakia, Moravia existed between the time of the great Slavic migration (A.D. 450—550) and the annexation of the territory by the Bohemian Empire (A.D. 973). Although nothing but foundations are left of its architecture and mere pieces of its wall paintings survive, numerous examples of its handicrafts are extant. These latter artifacts show a remarkable maturity and technical expertise.

It is interesting to look at Moravian handicrafts from a purely aesthetic perspective, seeing them as beautiful and accomplished works of art, but it is even more intriguing to view them in light of the activities, experiences, politics, and cultural influences that resulted in their creation. For they did not simply appear out of nowhere; nor were they the random products of chance historical events. Rather, they reflect a complex synthetic process that took place over a span of centuries. It is this synthetic process, as illustrated by the plates, that we will be discussing here.

During the great Slavic migration, which lasted for a full century, it was not uncommon for whole towns and tribes to move from place to place. Thus it should come as no surprise that many of the Moravian artifacts found to date bear the stamps of several cultures — some of which the Moravians encountered directly, and some of which they learned about in other ways.

To begin with, the Moravians were undoubtedly aware of the ancient Greco-Roman civilization. They knew of it from the remains of military camps and the pillaged ruins of Roman towns in Pannonia and Noricum, and also from the revived Byzantine Empire, which stretched along the Adriatic coast and into northern Italy. Its influence can be seen in findings as diverse as the pair of silver and partially gilt helmets from Dolné Semerovce (plates 2 and 3) and the torso of an ivory pyxis from a looted prince's grave at Žuráň (plates 4—6). Another fragment of a similar Alexandrine pyxis, which was recently found in southwest Slovakia at an indisputably Old Slavic excavation site, gives credence to this assumption.

Various Germanic and nomadic tribes determined the political and cultural framework of Moravia's earliest history. Of particular interest, though, is the close relationship that the peoples of the territory apparently had with north Pontic groups, which were both genetically and ethnically heterogeneous and contained elements of Slavic as well as nomadic cultures. This relationship is embodied in a number of belt ornaments bearing engraved and beaten geometric decorations (plates 1, 8, and 9), patterns which depict the last stage of development in abstract animal and plant ornamentation. In these belt ornaments can also be seen vestiges of Greco-Roman traditions, especially in the stylized intertwined patterns and the combined metalwork and paste gemstone construction.

The women's jewelry, on the other hand — specifically the open bracelets and earrings (plates 10—22) — reflect both Byzantine and Black Sea traditions. These are most obvious in the crescent-shaped lower arcs and the star-shaped and globular pendants of the earrings. But by far the most stunning example of classical Byzantine beaten metal art found in Moravia is the silver bowl from Zemiansky Vrbovok (plate 23). The eight-petaled rosette at the bottom and the stylized tendrilous pattern below the brim are its most notable and characteristic features.

The articles described above (and those which we will discuss below) have caused us to revise our original opinion of the Moravians. In the past, before many of these items were found and studied, it was thought that their culture was very

primitive. Their strict funeral rites, which involved cremation, and the unfavorable soil conditions of the area, which had a deleterious effect on the semi-subterranean dwellings, gave the appearance of poverty and a lack of sophistication. One need only look at the artifacts, however, to realize that the Moravians had a highly developed culture which functioned on several levels.

The Middle Danube Bronzes

Although there are few written records of the political changes that shaped Moravia during the seventh century, we can see their effects in the objects that survive to the present day.

The revolt of the Slavic tribes under Samo, the defeat of Byzantium in 626, domestic strife, and the advance of the Bulgarians into the lower Danube region in 674 caused problems for the ruling khan dynasty. The resulting political and social changes affected both the form and the technique of Moravian handicrafts. For example, Byzantium stopped paying its traditional annual tribute to the khan dynasty. Perhaps because of this, the number of solitary princes' graves declined, and no more sets of gold jewelry and hammered fittings (plate 20) were created. Of greater importance is the fact that the silver industry was gradually replaced by an emphasis on cast bronze metalworking. The cast bronze industry eventually dominated the entire Carpathian basin and the east Alpine region as well as Moravia itself. Its precise origins are still a subject for debate among scholars.

Thematically speaking, the bronze pieces dating from this period reflect the heterogeneous heritage of the Hellenistic East along with Persian, early Christian, and Byzantine influences (plates 27–73). This is evident in the decoration of the belt ornaments, which show the Hellenistic-Scythian animal style, and in the individual fittings with human figures. The motifs of Nereid (plate 58) and of the Herculean tasks (plate 65) clearly point to late folk replicas of early Hellenistic artistic traditions. Also of interest are the Greco-Roman themes of circus fights (plate 64) and the figurative representations of the nomadic

4

shaman (plate 62). From the point of view of local traditions, however, the most important work is the large belt-end from Moravský Ján with the figure of the falconer (plate 66).

During the last third of the eighth century, geometric plant ornamentation dominated the belt mountings. That so much effort was expended on beautifying a single item of men's apparel — the belt — is noteworthy. The belt itself was once considered (and in some cultures is still considered) a social and cultural symbol of major proportions. Even today folk traditions within some areas hold that the belt has magical powers. In the case of the Moravians, an elaborately crafted belt with a decorative end attested to the high standing of its wearer in a semipatriarchial and semifeudal society.

In contrast, the women's jewelry created during this period shows little variety of form, and its unpretentious aesthetic charm is concentrated on the contrast between gilt bronze and colored glass stones (plates 67—73). Older artistic traditions are represented by round earrings with beads hanging from both their lower and upper arcs. During the second half of the eighth century, oval earrings made of shaped wire became popular, and these were decorated with pyramid- or cone-shaped glass pendants. Especially rare are earrings with pendants in the shape of grape clusters and those which feature S-shaped knots or spirals. The information gleaned from this meager selection of earrings is only slightly augmented by the staminate bracelets and small wheel-, belt-, or escutcheon-like rings occasionally decorated with glass stones.

The Development of the Moravian Style

The overthrow of the Avar Empire by the armies of Charles the Great and the Frankish occupation of Pannonia completely transformed the balance of power in the middle Danube region. One striking result of these changes was decline of the admirable cultural harmony that had existed in the Carpathian basin, Moravia, and lower Austria and had been symbolized by the cast bronze industry. This interethnical ex-

pression of the pre-Great Moravian emphasis on artistic handicrafts did not die out suddenly, however. Its reverberations
were still being felt as late as the first decades of the ninth
century.

But the style of the ornamentation itself began to change
near the end of the eighth century. For example, the original
plant ornamentation of the cast bronzes was gradually en-
riched by various technical and formal elements. The plastic
openwork plant ornamentation was primarily used to decorate
the large belt-ends and clasps, while a more planar style of
engraved lines was used on the lateral mountings of the belt
sets (plates 83—87).

A fine example of this developmental process is the belt set
from Šaľa found at grave number 152 (plates 83 and 86). In the
decorative frame of the large belt-end can be seen an effective
new rendition of the ancient tree-of-life motif in which typical
lily flowers, with two bending slender petals flanking a pointed
central one, alternate with heteromorphic leaves on opposing
branches. The motif of conversely joined lily palmettes also
decorates the openwork hinge plate of the clasp, while the other
mountings on the belt are ornamented with completely different designs.

The shape of the mountings is as significant as their
ornamentation. By the second half of the eighth century,
belt-ends usually took one of two forms: the tongue or the
escutcheon. In both cases the two-part hinged construction
remained, but the mainly circular appendages diminished in
size, lost their original function, and eventually only supplemented the bearing mountings. These gradual changes can
be seen in the artifacts found at Šaľa (plates 83 and 84). In the
belt-end, the slim tongue-shaped mounting with its slightly
narrowed base moves fluently into the small semicircular
appendage. The two flat discs with punched dots surrounded
by a narrow frame repeat the tree-of-life pattern, making full
use of palmette elements and the three-petaled fleur-de-lis of
the chalice and crown. The escutcheon-shaped eyelet mountings feature simplified renditions of the palmette flower seen on
the hinge plate of the clasp.

In spite of the fact that the Šaľa belt set clearly indicates

the use of two disparate techniques, the mountings illustrate a harmonious artistic whole. From this we can assume that they emanated from the workshop of a single craftsman.

SASSANID AND ISLAMIC INFLUENCES

The origin of the palmette decoration on a dotted background can be traced directly to Sassanid and early Islamic artistic handicrafts. Scholars do not agree as to the individual or culture that acted as the intermediary in this process. Some think that the naturalization of this new style was directly connected with the same group of workshops that produced the gold vessels from the famous treasure of Sînnicolaul-Mare. On the other hand, those items might have been part of the khan treasure that was buried either during the Frankish invasion of 791—795 or later during the Bulgarian occupation of the Tisza region. Unfortunately, a stylistic and iconographic analysis of this type of ornamentation does not yield sufficiently reliable data with which to place it chronologically. Thus, this question is the subject of great controversy.

What is certain is the fact that these motifs were secondarily derived from a late-Sassanid environment, and therefore stem from the same circles as the themes for the planar ornamentation of the Šaľa bronzes. This decorative style was to disappear for a while and be revived on another type of ornamentation in the first decades of the ninth century.

In the collection of relics taken from a Blatnica prince's grave (plate 82) we can see palmette and semipalmette patterns on traditional escutcheon fittings and plastically modeled pendants in the shape of festooned clusters. From grave number 821 at Mikulčice and grave number 778 at Holiare come artifacts bearing a branching, asymmetrical arabesque pattern which covers the whole of the decorated area of the cast metal belt-ends. The belt-ends themselves are shaped like a horse's head (plate 80) or a boar's head (plate 81). These fittings remind us not only of the well-known protomas of Scythian artistic handicrafts, but also of the Sassanid reliefs which appeared much later in time on the square stone plates from Damghan.

We can trace the revival of the ancient animal symbols on

other metal ornaments as well — such as the openwork bronze fitting from Mikulčice which features the image of a griffin wrestling with a dragon (plate 79). The source of this ancient artistic transcription of the eternal struggle between good and evil is confirmed in this piece not only by the stylistic conception itself but also by the existence of yet another artifact with an incontestably Sassanid motif (plate 101). Although the image of facing peacocks guarding a stylized tree of life eventually passed into Christian iconography, its oriental origins are made apparent on the fragment of the Mikulčice belt-end by the symbolic ribbons around the peacocks' necks and by the presence of the palmettes on the dotted background.

While the attempt at combining palmette ornamentation with the plastic reliefs of cast bronze resulted in some unusual effects, it essentially weakened the original aesthetic charm inherent in both techniques. This can be seen in the belt-end from Modrá (plate 96) that was found in grave number 22 near one of the oldest Moravian churches with an oblong apse. The massive modeled frame of this belt-end is decorated in strained relief with alternating oval arcs and pairs of drop-shaped leaves which touch each other at their widened ends. At the lateral edge of the frame is a continuous intertwining chain of flowers, clearly a descendant of the three-leaved palmette. The narrowed inner area of the belt-end features five garland-like clusters set against an openwork background, a device similar to that found on the hinges on the Blatnica fittings. In spite of the pleasing effect produced when light plays across the surface of this piece, the overall impression is one of crudeness, and the item as a whole falls far short of the elegance of the Šaľa belt-end (plate 86). We should not, however, dwell too long on the imperfections of the Modrá relic; it is more profitable to look upon this object as signifying the emergence of new artistic trends.

CAROLINGIAN ELEMENTS AND TRACES OF INSULAR ART

The era which began while the traditions of the cast bronze industry were fading is documented only by a few imported objects. Among these is the gilded bronze ornament found at Hradec near Prievidza (plate 100). It features two escutcheon

shapes joined by a vertical partition with three openings for threads. Its overall rectangular shape derives from the four rings at the corners which were used for fastening the ornament to the belt. The decoration on the escutcheons consists of extremely stylized figures of birds facing backwards; the bird on the right side is turned 180 degrees away from the one on the left.

This piece is similar in some ways to metalwork objects found in Perugia and Ascoli-Piceno. On these latter works the animal decoration and the imitations of geometric plaiting point unambiguously to the insular influence of Irish and Scottish art. (This theory was first posited in the late 1950's by J. Cibulka, but it did not win much acceptance at that time.) The chalice of Tassilo from Kremsmünster is the most famous example of how pronounced this influence was in the Bavarian Danube region.

The Hradec belt ornament also features a typical notching technique. The gradual change from planar decoration to notching was a direct result of the Carolingian culture's stylistic development. In the case of the Hradec mounting, we can take this one step further and consider the effects of middle Danube traditions. The positioning of the stylized bird figures and the geometric S-shaped design are both reminiscent of the way in which griffins were portrayed on the large belt-end from grave number 67 at Šebastovce (plates 35—37). This connection begins to make more sense when we learn that the Bavarian prince Tassilo had relations with the Alpine Slavs and the Avars of the middle Danube.

The Hradec metalwork, which can be viewed as typologically unique within the Moravian territory, is less conspicuously beautiful with regard to form than other similar artifacts but nevertheless is charming in a novel way. Today it is generally acknowledged that the gilded bronze belt-end found at grave number 223/51 in the Staré Město churchyard (plate 94) belongs to this same group of Carolingian-influenced artifacts. The Staré Město belt-end features a notched decoration in which two pairs of entwined snakes form distinct heart shapes. In some ways, this piece is more reflective of Greco-Roman traditions than of insular animal motifs, but it still represents the final phase of the early Carolingian handicrafts, at least as they appeared within Moravia.

The bronze shield-like belt-end from Mikulčice (plate 93) poses similar analytical problems. Its shape is similar to that of pieces we have already been able to place within the purview of the insular style, but the origins of its rooflike arched obverse with deep triangular radiating grooves are more difficult to ascertain. J. Poulik has proposed that this artifact was the product of a native craftsman from the turn of the ninth century who was familiar with the products of the Irish and Scottish workshops, and that seems reasonable. In fact, his theory is supported by other items found at grave number 108 near the second Mikulčice church, including objects from the late horizon of the middle Danube cast bronzes.

Early cultural connections with the Carolingians are apparent in other metal fittings with notched decorations from Modrá, Staré Město, and Pohansko near Břeclav. Even though these fittings are of various shapes and served several different functions, they have in common their symmetrical composition and extremely geometric ornamentation. On the oval loop from grave number 114/15 from Staré Město (plate 97, above), for example, the focal point of the pattern rests in the center of the decorated area, out of which spreads the design of conversely oriented voluted chalices and heart-shaped tendrils. In contrast, the palmette anthemion of the Staré Město belt-end from grave number 190/50 (plate 97, below) is more reminiscent of the stylized tree-of-life motif. Here the notching technique loses its depth and sharpness and the forms are rounded; thus, only the overall shape of this object and the method by which it was attached to the belt relate it to previous pieces.

The fundamental significance of the artifacts discussed here rests not in their problematic nature but in the fact that they illustrate the first artistically recorded contacts that the Moravians had with the Carolingians. When the items were actually placed in the graves is not that important. Their rarity can be seen as testifying to the declining influence of the Irish and Scottish missions in central Europe and can also be viewed as proving that the political orientation of the Moravians had not yet solidified by the end of the eighth century.

THE BLATNICA HORIZON

The ensuing decades witnessed radical changes in the so-called Blatnica-Mikulčice horizon. By now Moravian craftsmen had a wide range of influences from which to choose, and they were able to select elements from the ornamental content of Carolingian art which suited their aesthetic needs and traditions. We can identify differences, for example, in the ways in which Moravian craftsmen and those from Pribina's Nitra expressed themselves. One reason for this is that the style of cast bronzes was more deeply rooted in Slovakia than in Moravia.

Consider, for instance, the relics found in a prince's grave in Turčianska Blatnica. These embody certain definite Carolingian elements. The most interesting item in this collection is the strikingly decorated sword (plate 88). The head, handle, and transverse of the hilt are all plated with gilded bronze and inset with silver. On the handle, perpendicular rows of flat ovals with silver hammered stripes are interwoven with two ribbons of silver stripes, while the space formed by this pattern is filled with eight-pointed stars that give the impression of a notching technique. Even the deliberately distributed ends of the threads form an organic part of the whole and contribute to its colorful, plastic effect.

A row of larger and smaller oval-shaped human masks winds around the handle above the transverse and below the head. With minor variations, this geometric scheme is repeated on the transverse of the hilt. On the head itself, the central row of concave rhomboids is especially notable, as are the narrow ribbons with their continuously joined S-shaped spirals. This rich geometric ornamentation can be compared with the decoration found on the sword from Vaage in Norway; H. Arbman believes that both examples were native imitations of Carolingian swords.

INSPIRATION FROM THE ADRIATIC COAST

Although it is interesting to determine the status of the Blatnica sword within the context of European handicrafts created during approximately the same period, it is more useful to study its position within the Moravian environment.

To begin with, its human mask motif is highly unusual. Animal masks were more common in the north; in fact, human masks appeared only in Longobardic Italy on straight-armed Greek crosses and some secular objects. In the Christian Museum in Brescia, for example, is a bronze disc-shaped plaque whose edges are decorated by twenty concentrically oriented human masks. These are notably similar in form to the ones which ring the gilded phalera of a horse's halter found at grave number 10 at Žitavská Tôň (plate 99). This phalera is quite exceptional, and it is likely that it originated in the south. No direct connection between this piece and the Blatnica sword can be drawn, but it is likely that they, together with other objects, hastened the naturalization of the motif within the Moravian territory.

In a wider context, the figurative motifs on two cross-shaped ornaments and two key-shaped belt-ends from the Blatnica horse's harness (plate 82) are linked with the Longobardic region. Both the mirrored design of the oblong areas of decoration and the outstretched arms of the frontally modeled human figures seem strikingly analogous to the metal fittings from the seventh-century Longobardic burial grounds at Nocera Umbra and Mazzoglio. While the Italian artifacts demonstrate a planar version of the theme via the niello technique, the Blatnica collection features plastic relief ornamentation, which can be seen to correspond with the traditions of cast bronzes.

THE MIKULČICE STYLE

The remolding power of the native environment and the aesthetic taste of the early Moravians are most evident in a group of relics which represent the Mikulčice style of artistic handicrafts. While an analysis of the technique, form, or ornamental motifs would lead us back to specific forms of late Greco-Roman art, even exact interpretations of the available data would not help us to grasp the essence of this style and its meaning. For in spite of the apparent commonness of the individual formal and ornamental aspects of these early Moravian objects, they nevertheless exhibit a unique harmonic sense that warrants admiration.

The heavily gilded spurs (plate 89) with their parabolically shaped arms divided into casketlike sections are, it must be admitted, imitations of Carolingian models; nowhere else but in Moravia, however, are they found with mask or semipalmette ornamentation. And this artistic design was certainly deliberate; the same combination of human masks with a pointed-leaf semipalmette and a horizontal cross was regularly used for men's ornaments such as spurs, belt-ends, clasps, and loops. This is documented by findings from grave number 44 near the second Mikulčice church and from grave number 50 beside the rotunda with two apses (plates 90 and 91).

In grave number 44, two gilded hammered buttons with a palmette design formed against a dotted background into a heart-shaped meander were found (plate 92). The origins of this type of ornamentation can doubtless be traced back to the last horizon of the middle Danube cast bronzes. At one time, scholars were surprised to find such typically Great Moravian decorations as those which were demonstrated on the buttons; they eventually attributed them to the second half of the ninth century. Recent findings at Mikulčice justify this dating and may be compared with the cast escutcheon-shaped fittings of the Blatnica type.

Interestingly, there are very few pieces of women's jewelry among the early Moravian relics of the Mikulčice style, which reached the climax of its development in the second half of the ninth century. This lack is somewhat compensated for by a plenitude of cast belt-ends. These pieces are unusually massive; both their shape and their decoration can be seen as antithetical to the slim belt-ends of the nomads. It seems as if the whole political attitude of the old Moravians was concentrated into this single artistic and ideological symbol.

Of course, not all of the massive belt-ends discovered thus far come from the early Mikulčice horizon. But it is clear that the first ones date from this period. A superb example is the gilded silver belt-end (plates 102 and 103) from grave number 100 near the second Mikulčice church. Its short, wide tongue shape reflects Carolingian influences, as do the five thread holes at the neck. Some scholars have assumed that the oval marginal area of the obverse side, decorated with rough cast granulation, derived from the belt-ends of the latest Avar-Slavic horizon. But the five plastically raised rhombic leaves decorated with niello on the circumference force us to reconsider this opinion. It is likely that the craftsman who made them had other examples before him, an idea which is supported by their unusual thickness.

Although most of these belt-ends were cast in one piece, hollow specimens do exist; in one (plate 117), an almandine nucleus was used to symbolize Christ's blood. From this we can posit the theory that the leaf-like shapes on the circumference of this and other belt-ends were intended to serve as imitations of the hinge clasps which originally closed typical two-part reliquaries. This explanation simplifies the stylistic origin of these belt-ends, which then cease to be hybrid creations, and indicates the source for most of the engraved figurative motifs on their flat sides.

In some cases the relation between the symbolic meaning of the motifs used on both sides of the belt-ends is obvious; in others further research will have to be done before any real conclusions can be drawn. In selected pieces (plates 102 and 103), the decorations of the two sides are clearly related. Both the typical mask-like motif in the upper part of the decorated area and the representation of an eye in the lower are thematically connected with the figure of a suppliant on the reverse side. If the inspiration for this piece stemmed from a reliquary, then the figure with a stylized halo around his head and a straight-armed Greek cross on his chasuble no doubt represents a suppliant saint and the whole artistic conception points to the Coptic-Byzantine area. These motifs, which seem so artistically remote, may have penetrated the Moravian territory during the missionary activities of the Aquila patriarchate.

Also of interest is the ornamentation on a gilded bronze belt-end (plates 104 and 105) found at grave number 240 near the apse of the Mikulčice triple-aisle basilica (plate 180). Its emphatically designed obverse is cast in a deep-cut notching pattern, while its circumference is decorated with an extremely schematized plant pattern. The rounded holes were probably filled with colored glass flowers. The border features raised symbolic hinge clasps, while at the center is a stylized image of a frog seen from above. This combined metal and colored glass construction clearly points to the west. On the reverse, the deliberately simplified engraving of a man holding a labarum in his right hand and a drinking horn in his left can be seen as representing both power and rank. The incorporation of such evident symbolism into this piece was anything but accidental.

This mosaic of heterogeneous impulses, this eager acceptance of all positive values tempered by an uncompromising assessment of their real contribution to the development of Moravian culture — such was the character of Mojmir's territory before Rastislav came to power and the Byzantine missionaries arrived.

The Great Moravian Synthesis

The findings which comprise the basic collection of Great Moravian artistic handicrafts date mainly from the ninth century, although some originate from the first half of the tenth. In the previous section we paid special attention to the narrow selection of Mikulčice-style relics for a number of reasons. Specifically, in addition to possessing interesting stylistic features, those pieces can be seen as chronologically outlining the artistic expression of the inhabitants prior to the arrival of the Byzantine missionaries. In fact, however, there is no sharp distinction in form between these artifacts and the ones which date from the second half of the ninth century; apparently the Carolingian ornamental elements were simply replaced by others.

THE STRENGTHENING OF BYZANTINE INFLUENCES

The massive belt-ends can again be viewed as classic examples. For instance, the large silver belt-end (plates 111 and 112) found near the triple-aisle basilica exactly repeats the design of the bronze piece with the suppliant (plates 102 and 103). On the obverse side is a wide border surrounding a central area divided into halves by a double row of pearls. The number of the fastening threads has increased from five to seven, as has the number of imitation hinge clasps on the circumference. In this object both Byzantine and oriental influences are evident. The decoration of the border — which repeats a motif of semicircular decorations with their rounded edges turned inward and is rendered in filigree chain work — is certainly oriental. Its equivalent linear version can be seen on the round clasps discovered at the Longobard burial ground in Castel Trosino. On the rough, dotted surface of the reverse side of the belt-end, in complete harmony with the obverse, there is a stylized tree of life whose symmetrically arranged palmette twigs are surrounded by a double entwining ribbon.

Evidence of a divergence from this basic scheme is found on the elaborate belt-ends from grave number 490 near the triple-aisle basilica in Mikulčice (plate 113) and from grave number 96/AZ in Staré Město near Uherské Hradiště (plate 116). Neither piece features the traditional massive border on the obverse, and the close semiotic relationship between the decoration of the obverse and reverse sides has also disappeared. The decoration, however, is enhanced by the presence of semiprecious stones.

The hollow Mikulčice piece is made of thin silver plate, and its obverse is covered by a dense network of finely interwoven silver threads. This latticework is bordered by a somewhat wider rufflike band, and similar bands stretch from the corners toward the center of a pinkish opaque glass stone, connecting it to a smaller oval carnelian. The primitive engraved figure of a four-legged animal on the surface of the stone could not have been executed by the original artist; it too obviously detracts from the intended contrast between the broken-light effects of the latticework and the serene tones of the centrally placed stones. In fact, a laboratory examination has revealed that a figure of Mercury was engraved on the underside of the carnelian. This testifies not only to the Greco-Roman origin of the stone but also to the deliberate exclusion of the surface engraving from the primary decorative design.

The latticework technique in itself was not unusual in Moravia. It can also be seen on the double-surfaced buttons and earrings (plates 128 and 129). We can consider this technique to be the product of a local craftsman, a claim which is supported by the figure of a suppliant on the dotted reverse side of a belt-end from Mikulčice (plate 114). Partly engraved and partly hammered, it contains precise details we have not seen before. The bell-shaped, open, twice-girded coat and the wide trousers tucked into soft boots are reminiscent of the Ukrainian national costume; J. Poulik was probably right in assuming that this was also the national costume of the Old Moravians.

THE FUSION OF FOREIGN INFLUENCES

The origin and style of the silver belt-end from Staré Město (plate 116) has been the subject of controversy for several decades. In a recent study, T. Capelle came to the conclusion that its obverse side, decorated with filigree work and cabochons, reflects the Carolingian traditions, while the partially engraved, partially pressed palmette ornamentation on the dotted background of the reverse side (plate 115) resembles the silver plates of the Old Hungarian reticules. But does the stylistic contrast of the decoration really signify two different sources of inspiration?

To answer this question, we must take into account the syncretic character of Carolingian art, which was not limited to a mere revival of Greco-Roman traditions. The back cover of the book of the Gospels preserved in the monastery in St. Gallen, for example, reveals some interesting connections. Its central ivory plate with an engraved image of Christ is considered to be the work of the monk Tutila. This plate is set in a beaten silver frame whose decoration bears surprising resemblance to the basic scheme of the ornamentation of the Staré Město belt-end. Five cabochons set in a similar way on a square field alternate with crossed palm leaves, and these are supplemented by a fine geometrical tendrillar motif made of thin wire. Only the typical punched dots are missing: these, of course, would have given the whole frame a distinct oriental appearance. The patterns on the obverse of the Staré Město belt-end (the lyre- and chalice-shaped and semicircular patterns with loops turned inward) are produced in chain filigree work and create an oriental setting for the symmetrically

placed semiprecious stones. This setting, though unusual, does not conflict with the stylistically related ornamentation of the reverse side. In other words, this artifact was hardly the result of simply copying two heterogeneous forms. Instead, it symbolized the unification of two distinct ornamental principles at a new level of concept and feeling. It is clear that the unknown craftsman knew what he was doing.

IMPORTED ARTIFACTS AND STYLES

Thus far we have been able to claim with relative certainty the native origins of the findings discussed. We cannot do the same, however, in the case of another group of relics that are alien in both form and technique.

One such relic — which was certainly imported — is the unique gold belt-end (plate 117) found at a filled-in grave, plundered long ago, near the triple-aisle basilica in Mikulčice. Its main feature is a carefully polished dark red almandine. This is set in a gold mounting, held by lily-shaped teeth, and bordered by little granulated pyramids. The neck is decorated with two thin wreaths of real pearls joined by a fine wire, which in itself indicates that the owner of this valuable piece was one of the Great Moravian nobility. The techniques used in its production and its unusual shape combine to suggest that this was a genuine Byzantine import.

In the same burial ground, in grave number 433, a much simpler variation of a belt-end with a gem was found (plate 120). The polished side of the gem, again facing downward, is set in silver. A close examination of the stone reveals quite a surprise: on its reverse is a finely engraved picture of three different heads joined into a single whole, visible from different angles. The bearded head, as it turns out, is that of Zeus. This determination is given credence by the presence of the second emphatically designed head — that of Zeus's sacred bird, the eagle. The third profile has been identified as a self-portrait of the famous early sculptor Feidias. (Interestingly, this was not the only time when Feidias imposed his rather unusual "signature" on a work of art. He once smuggled his self-portrait onto a copy of Pallas Athena's shield — an action which resulted in his prosecution and imprisonment.) The similarity of the two

portraits — the one found on the Mikulčice belt-end, and the one found on the shield — excited classical archaeologists, who were led to this discovery by the initials of the Latinate form of the artist's name: Phidias.

The Moravians had no idea of the exceptional value of this late Greco-Roman engraving, and we cannot blame them for trying to cover it up by turning the stone over. They made use of gems from ancient jewelry in more than one instance. A pendant found in grave number 3 at Modrá (plate 118) contains yet another example of this technique. Into a silver frame with a loop, which is decorated with a filigree lyre-shaped design on the reverse, they set a carnelian with a Hellenistic engraving of Eros leaning toward a cock.

NATIVE ARTIFACTS

A number of complex relationships exist between artistic expression and the environment and between artistic expression and societal ideologies. Clarifying these has long been the task of art historians, many of whom have chosen to devote their efforts to studying the development of monumental art. While architectural remains can certainly reveal a great deal about a people and its way of life, they unfortunately tend to suffer the ravages of time more seriously than do artifacts. In the case of Moravia, jewelry and belt-ends were often buried with the dead and in this way were preserved for centuries; their buildings, however, simply decayed over the years. Thus we can glean little real information from what is left of their monumental art.

Neither the uncovered foundations of Great Moravian sacred and secular buildings (plates 179—186) nor the surviving fragments of wall paintings are able to provide us with much useful data. Regardless of how carefully archaeologists and scholars try to reconstruct these edifices, we will never be able to determine their precise original appearance. We can make certain assumptions as to their origin and function, but that is about all we can do. So we are forced to turn away from these foundations and wall paintings in dismay and focus instead on those relics which have been able to resist the gnawing tooth of the centuries.

Of particular interest are the crosses. From an artistic point of view, they signify far more than the probability that those with whom they were buried were Christians. In fact, some crosses may have been merely decorative. For example, the cast bronze cross found at the fifth church in Mikulčice apparently came from a horse's harness, if the thread openings are any indication (plate 123). This particular piece, then, may not have been an object of worship or even of undue reverence. Similarly, the relief mask decoration likely had no inherent religious meaning; a comparable mask can be seen on an earlier phalera from Žitavská Tôň (plate 99). In other words, this piece seems to have resulted from the chance combination of two artistically disparate elements into a single and apparently united whole.

This Mikulčice cross differs from examples found at Blatnica and Pobedim and even from others discovered at Mikulčice itself (plates 121 and 124) with respect to the three-cornered endings of its arms. These, together with the projecting rings for threads, give it an unreal fragility and make it nearer in shape and appearance to the contemporary crosses of Byzantine origin. The assumption that this relic dates from the beginning of the ninth century is in full accord with its stylistic and iconographical markings.

Two lead pendant crosses from grave number 467 in Dolní Věstonice may have originated slightly later in time. These, together with a silver reliquary in the shape of a missal, form the main ornaments on a necklace of heteromorphic glass and lead beads (plate 125). No other artifacts found so far have characteristics that are analogous to the crosses' short, wide arms with arched bases, but the lyre-shaped designs at their center may indicate that these are native products.

The great majority of the crosses discovered to date, however, are clearly foreign imports which were brought into Moravia by missionaries from outside its borders. Consider, for example, the silver pendant cross found in a plundered grave at Mikulčice (plate 126). The relief figure of the crucified Christ wearing a tunic with a wide border is at first glance reminiscent of the illustrative style of Coptic materials and limestone reliefs. In this case, however, such a superficial impression is

hardly sufficient, since the Coptic exiles left clear traces of their creative activity all the way from the Adriatic coast to Ireland. On this cross the closed halo emphatically separates the head of Christ from his own body and transforms it into a mask whose chiseled-out eyes give it a striking expression. This ornamentally conceived disintegration, with particular emphasis on the masklike head, is not the chance product of an unknown craftsman but rather is based on the traditions of insular art. The cross may be only a remote continental imitation of Old Irish artistic handicrafts, but from the point of view of style it undoubtedly belongs to the horizon which was directly influenced by the work of the Irish and Scottish missionaries.

The bronze crosses from Mača near Sereď (plate 127) and from Trnovec nad Váhom (plate 122) are of distinctly Byzantine origin, even though excavational circumstances place them at the beginning of the tenth century. The Mača cross deserves attention both because of its artistic form and because of its iconographic content. On it three framed figures placed one above the other have been engraved with remarkably firm lines. In spite of their schematism, they are a concrete example of how even a simple planar frontal view can achieve an expression of great spirituality. All three of the figures are women with long hair. If the suppliant woman holding a palm branch in one hand and an unidentified fruit in the other is the Virgin Mary, then the other two can be assumed to be Mary Cleophas and Mary Magdalene.

The three Marys began appearing together in Christian iconography at a very early date. We know, for example, of a particular wall painting that decorated the baptistry in Dura-Europos until the town was occupied and destroyed by the Parthians in 265. On the Mača cross, they are depicted on what is probably the reverse side of a two-sided reliquary, the obverse showing a picture of Christ. The whole therefore symbolizes not only the crucifixion but also — through the picture of the three Marys, one of whom holds a palm branch — the resurrection and the belief in eternal life. In other words, it represents all of the fundamental articles of the Christian faith.

In comparison with this simple but exceptional piece, the Trnovec cross-shaped reliquary is rather ordinary (plate 122). The semirelief, semiengraved pictures of Christ on the one side and Mary the suppliant on the other are frankly mediocre. In spite of the Greek initials on the transverse arms of the reverse side, we cannot rule out the possibility that this was only a native imitation of a more valuable Byzantine work.

THE SKILL OF NATIVE CRAFTSMEN

The extent of the apotropaic or religious significance of the motifs present on Moravian belt-ends and crosses was influenced to some extent by the functions which these objects were intended to perform. Of course, the Old Moravians used secular motifs as well. An especially beautiful example of this is the most outstanding work of Great Moravian cold metalwork found to date: a beaten silver plaque from grave number 15 in Staré Město (plate 131). The picture of a rider — a falconer — against a background of finely worked circles is designed in the classic heraldic style of post-Sassanid Islamic art and features a cleverly emphasized contrast between the realistically modeled figure of the horse and the extremely stylized clothing of the rider. To our knowledge, stylistically and compositionally close analogies to this falconer are found only on oriental silks. But the plastic, grooved border of the plaque indicates that its immediate source of inspiration may have been medallions from the silver or gold containers of the type discovered at Sînnicolaul-Mare. The costume of the rider is surprisingly similar to that of the suppliant on the Mikulčice belt-end (plate 114). Unless both examples are copies of oriental objects, it can be assumed that the rider's costume is in fact that of a Great Moravian nobleman.

Another very interesting motif is the figure of a kneeling archer engraved on a double-sided horn disc which was found in grave number 251 near the triple-aisle Mikulčice basilica (plates 132 and 133). On the obverse side of this disc the artist has portrayed a fight between a saurian — perhaps a crocodile — and some kind of hoofed animal. Although a similarly depicted figure of an archer can also be found on a Byzantine ivory horn in the collection in the Jászberény Museum in

Hungary, we cannot consider the origin of this ornament as solved.

As was shown in a recent study, the motif of a kneeling archer does not have its source in a nomadic environment, for it is found in the same form on the central Gallic terre sigillate and also appears as a popular decorative feature in Byzantine iconography. If one of the animals struggling on the obverse side of the disc really is a crocodile, we can perhaps begin to trace this piece back to a Coptic environment. This theory is supported by the series of little round holes along the raised edge, which gives the illusion of a row of pearls shown in the negative. An engraving technique of this type, and the cutting-out of the background to give positive contours to the figurative ornamentation, are typically Coptic.

The practice of carving bones or antlers was widespread throughout Great Moravia. But if we take a closer look at the carved and engraved ornamentation on a selection of bone objects and ornaments from various locales (plate 134), we soon discover that abstract geometrical patterns prevail — patterns which were probably used also in wood carving.

The most typical and, in a sense, the most beautiful native Moravian handicrafts that survive to the present day are the buttons and earrings (plates 135—52). In some of them — such as the buttons found in the grave treasures of the early Mikul-čice horizon — the revival of the old techniques of beaten metal, pressing, fine filigree, and granulation can be dated back to the beginning of the ninth century. Because the Mora-vians' love of massive cast ornaments faded slowly, however, these revived techniques became dominant again only in the second half of the ninth century. This development was prob-ably also connected with the fact that Moravia was entering a period of political and economic prosperity. The new technol-ogy was directly dependent on malleable precious metals, especially gold and silver.

It is remarkable how many gold pieces found their way into the graves of the urban centers in Great Moravia during this period. We know nothing about where this gold originated, but we do know that it was smelted and worked in native workshops. Traces of these have been uncovered by archaeologists both in Mikulčice and in Staré Město. The geographical locations at which the buttons and precious gold earrings were found also seem to verify that these objects were of native origin; the majority of them were unearthed in the empire's political, administrative, and trade centers.

The Moravian masters produced a wide variety of buttons from thin pressed metal. They worked primarily in copper and gold-plated metal, often silver, and only rarely in gold. The shape that the buttons most commonly took was a spherical one composed of two pressed hemispheres with hammered decorations on the surface. The ornamentation itself, which mainly consisted of a plant motif, was usually set either in a heart-shaped meander, framed with arcades, or in the center of medallions. The basic ornamental elements in the plant motif were the palmette fan shape and its derivatives, which sometimes developed into complicated symmetrical patterns reminiscent of various Mediterranean, Sassanid, and pre-Great Moravian Danubian ornamentations. In very few cases are animal motifs found in conjunction with the medallions or arcade-like frames. These are primarily stylized birds such as peacocks, doves, or even falcons. The frames, as well as the decorations themselves, are always plastically divided from the dotted background and serve as proof of the oriental origins of both the technique and ornamental conception used (plates 136 and 137).

Nearly all of the extant buttons, spherical or not, embody various combinations of granulation and filigree. Some are covered with granulated bosses, while others are decorated with intricate latticework that has been fused on, set with glass beads, or modeled into the shape of polygonal lanterns.

THE SIGNIFICANCE OF WOMEN'S JEWELRY

The largest single group of ornaments which were left behind by the Great Moravian Empire is made up of women's jewelry — earrings, necklaces, and rings (plates 139—64, 166—72, and 174—78). Of these, the earrings are considered to be the most important.

They are classified as grape-like, kettledrum (globular), or basket-, crescent-, or wand-shaped, depending on the style of

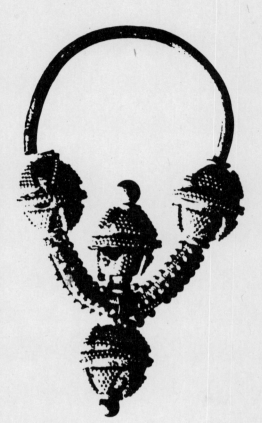

the pendant on the arc. Some of them, such as the grape-like pieces, can be directly traced back to Danubian folk ornamentation; only later did they reflect oriental Byzantine influences. Others, like the crescent-shaped ones, underwent a renaissance of sorts after a more than 150-year interval because of renewed cultural contacts with the Byzantines. This may explain why the art of earring-making reached its climax late — during the second half of the ninth century — although most of the styles were still being produced well into the tenth century and some even outlived the existence of Moravia as a political entity. The prevailing elements of their ornamentation were rough granulation in the shape of flat triangles, rhombuses, and plastic pyramids; occasionally finer granulation is seen. Real filigree is rare, and some particularly remarkable variations of the basic types appear only in the central strongholds of Great Moravia.

The same ornamental techniques are used on rings, on the metal beads of necklaces, and on the crescent-shaped pendants whose lunar designs are rife with the ancient symbolism of both eroticism and fertility.

As Moravia's political system and its internal balance of power gradually disintegrated, fewer symbols of class and military strength — e.g., elaborate belt-ends — were produced. (We know this because fewer of them have been found in graves dating from this period.) Interestingly, though, the amount of women's jewelry crafted at this time seems to have remained fairly constant. Perhaps Moravia's women became the defenders of their territory when the final sword fell from the powerless hands of the last weary warrior. Even if this seems rather far-fetched, it is true that a sort of "effeminization" of Moravian handicrafts occurred on the eve of the nation's impending destruction. And neither Přemysl's Bohemia nor Arpád's Hungary, both of which were just emerging, were at all interested in preserving Moravia's integrity or independence. We are lucky that the artifacts remain to reflect its long-lost glory.

THE PLATES
THE MAPS

The Slavs in the Sixth Century

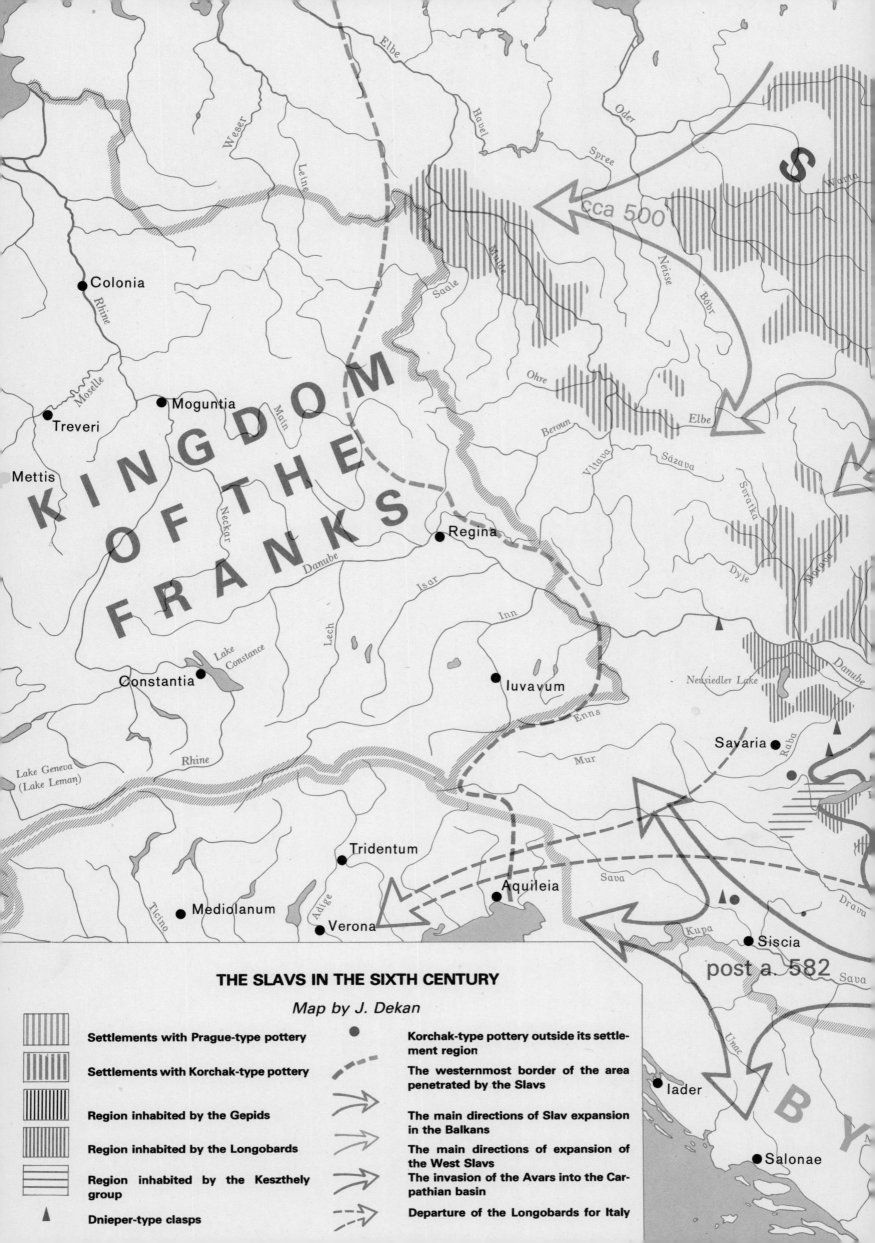

THE SLAVS IN THE SIXTH CENTURY

Map by J. Dekan

(vertical hatch)	Settlements with Prague-type pottery	●	Korchak-type pottery outside its settlement region
(hatch)	Settlements with Korchak-type pottery	– – –	The westernmost border of the area penetrated by the Slavs
(vertical hatch)	Region inhabited by the Gepids	→	The main directions of Slav expansion in the Balkans
(vertical hatch)	Region inhabited by the Longobards	→	The main directions of expansion of the West Slavs
(horizontal hatch)	Region inhabited by the Keszthely group	→	The invasion of the Avars into the Carpathian basin
▲	Dnieper-type clasps	⇢	Departure of the Longobards for Italy

Colonia

Moguntia

Treveri

Mettis

KINGDOM OF THE FRANKS

Regina

Constantia

Iuvavum

Lake Geneva (Lake Leman)

Tridentum

Mediolanum

Verona

Aquileia

Savaria

Neusiedler Lake

Siscia

post a. 582

Iader

Salonae

cca 500

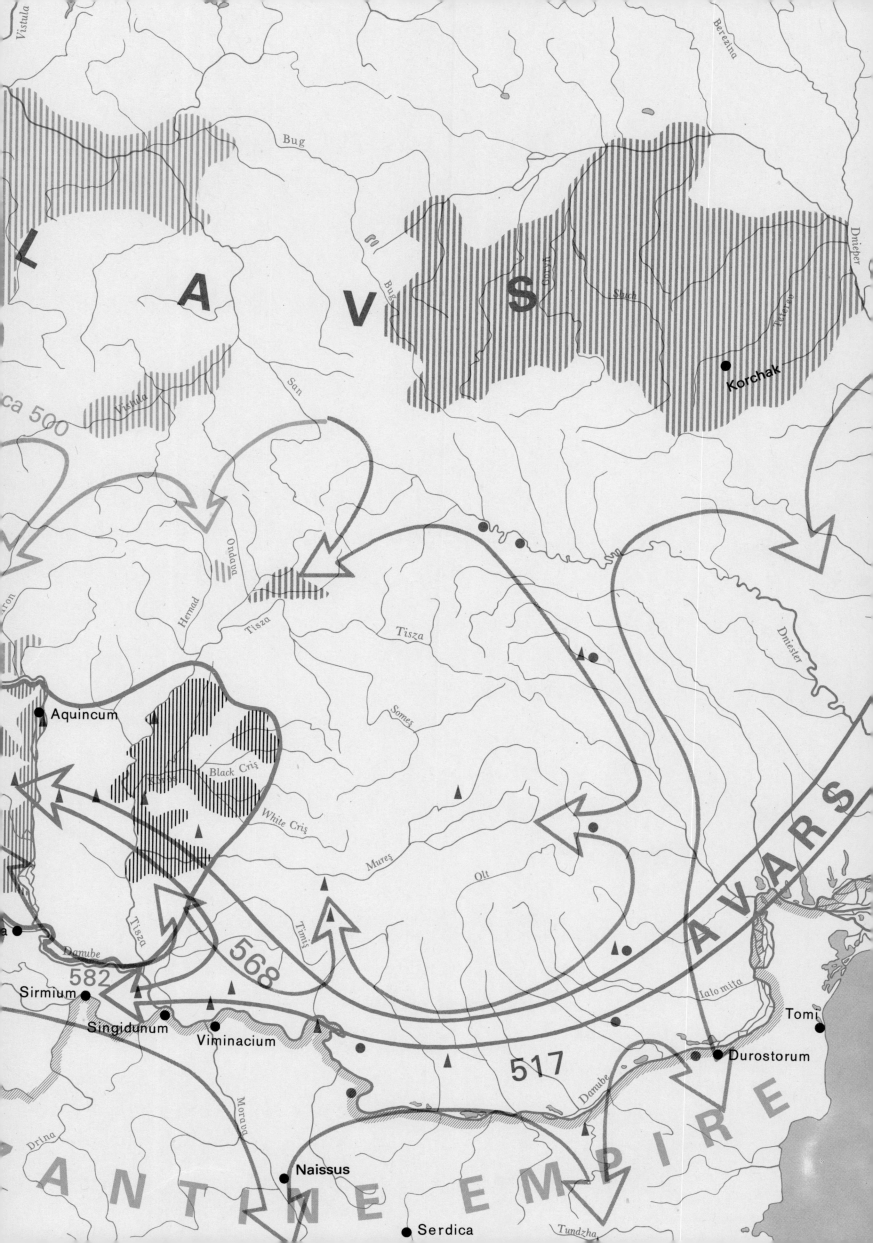

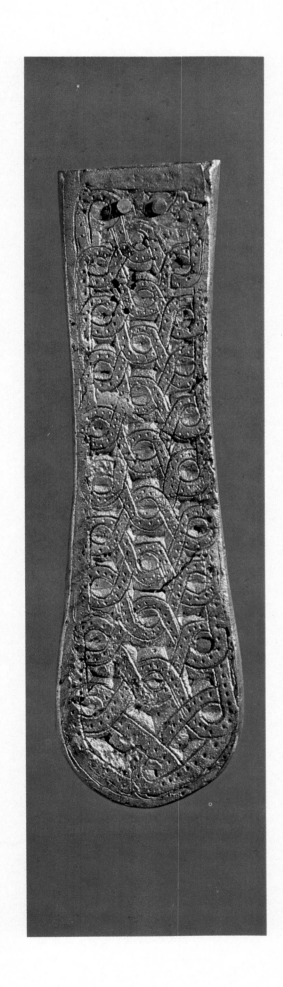

1. Silver belt-end with a hammered pattern in the form of interwoven figure eights. Holiare

2. *Silver and gold plated iron helmet of the Baldenheim type. Dolné Semerovce*

3. Gold-plated iron helmet of the Baldenheim type. Dolné Semerovce

7. Silver belt-end with an embossed zig-
zag pattern. Holiare

8. *Set of gilded belt ornaments with an embossed pattern and pale blue glass stones. Želovce*

9. *Set of gilded belt ornaments with embossed ornamentation and missing glass stones. Želovce*

10. *Silver earrings with globular pendants. Želovce*

11. *Gold earrings with hollow pendants decorated with granulation. Želovce*

12. *Silver earrings with globular pendants. Želovce*

13. *Silver earrings with a hollow sphere set with dark blue stones; the neck of the pendant is surrounded by globules. Holiare*

14. *Silver earring with unusual pendant. Holiare*

15. *Silver earrings with a richly molded neck and a pearl-shaped pendant studded with gilded decorations. Holiare*

16. *Bronze earrings with a crescent-shaped lower arc and globular ornamentation. Želovce*

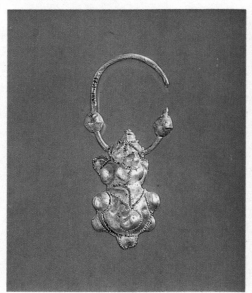

17. Beaten silver crescent-shaped earrings with star-like pendants. Želovce

19. Cast bronze crescent-shaped earrings with starlike pendants. Štúrovo

18. Beaten silver crescent-shaped earring with a starlike pendant. Holiare

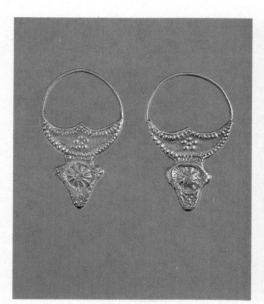

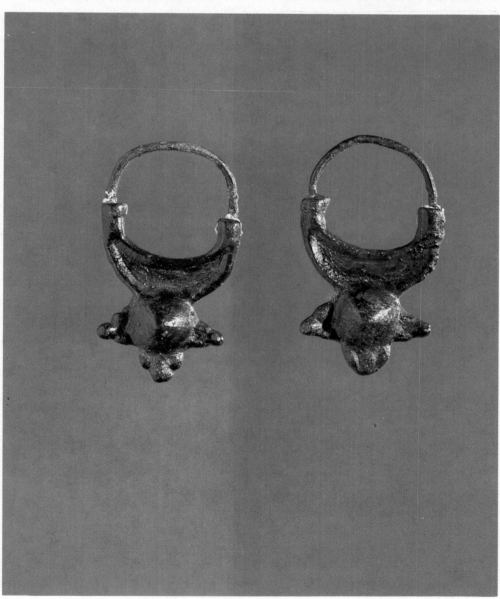

17   18

19

20. *Two square gold ornaments with a hammered design; gold two-part clasp set with dark blue oval stones.* Želovce

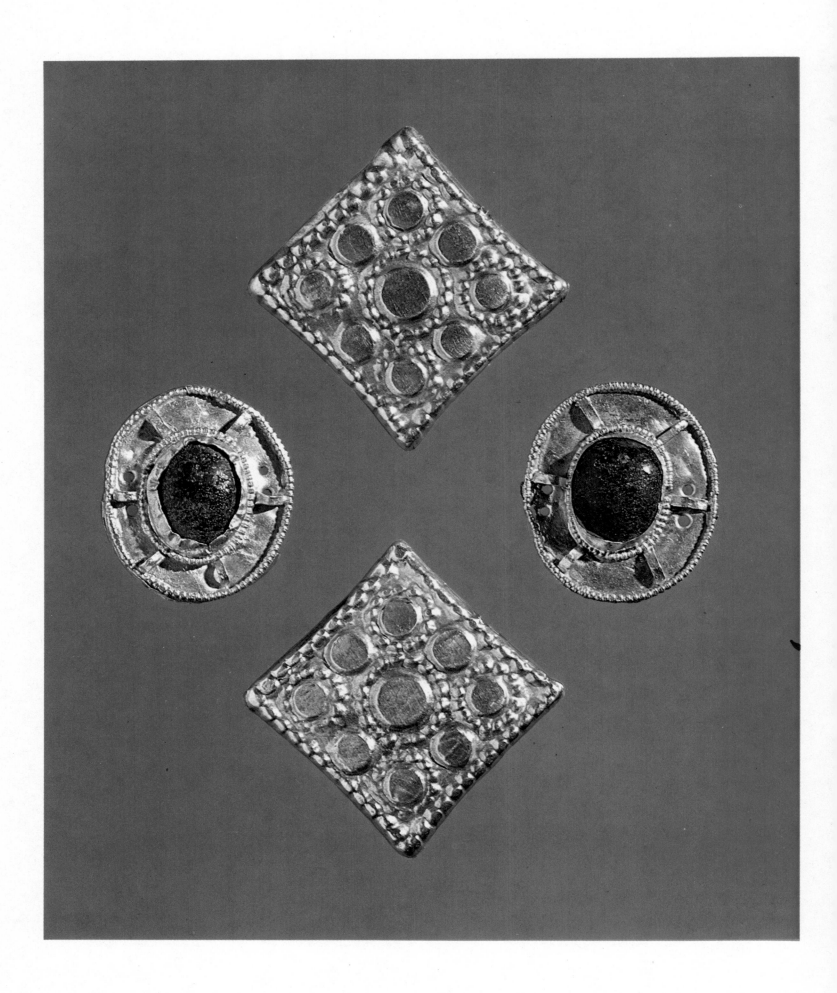

21. *Open silver bracelets; silver ring with a dark blue stone in a silver setting. Želovce*

22. *Gold earring with a cylindrical granulated pendant. Želovce*

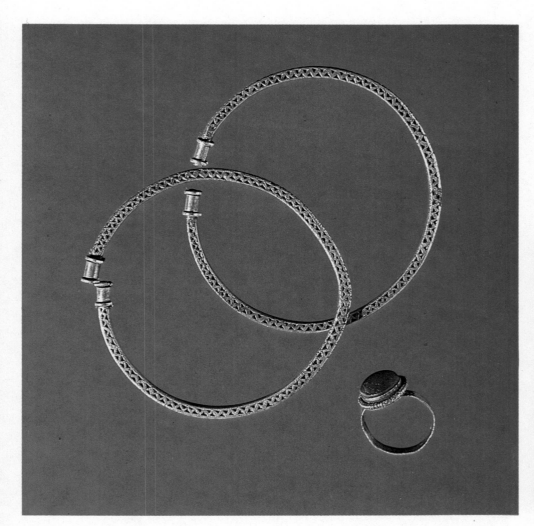

23. *Part of a silver treasure-trove: 1. silver hemispherical dish with embossed ornamentation; 2. silver chalice; 3. silver bracelet with hammered ornamentation; 4. silver bracelet with hammered ornamentation; 5. cast silver earring. Zemiansky Vrbovok*

24. *Pottery of the Prague type.*

25. *Pottery of the Tisza type from inhumation graves. Želovce*

26. *Hand-molded pottery from inhumation graves. Želovce*

The Territorial Development
of Great Moravia

SAXONY

LORRAINE

‡ Cologne

Hersfeld

Fulda

Frankfurt

‡ Mainz

Worms

FRANCONIA

Forchheim

ALEMANIA

Constance Lake

SORBS OR WENDS

L. Hradec

Prague

St. Kou

‡ Regensburg

Altaich

Passau †

BAVARIA

Freising †

Öttingen

Mattsee

‡ Salzburg

Kremsmünster

Traismauer

OSTMAR

CARINTHIA

Zr

FRIULIAN MARK

Cividale

Aquileia ‡

Venice

BYZANTINE EMPIRE

CROATI

S

THE TERRITORIAL DEVELOPMENT OF GREAT MORAVIA

from its unification as a state ± 830 A.D.
until Svätopluk's death 894 A.D.

Map by J. Dekan

Moravia under Mojmír and Rastislav.

Natural growth of Moravia after 874 A.D.

Svätopluk's conquests in the years 882–892 A.D.

Probable extent of Kocel's principality 861–874 A.D.

Territory temporarily tributary to Svätopluk.

The Avar province from 805–860 (?) A.D.

‡   Archbishoprics

†   Bishoprics

•   Other important places closely connected with the history of Great Moravia.

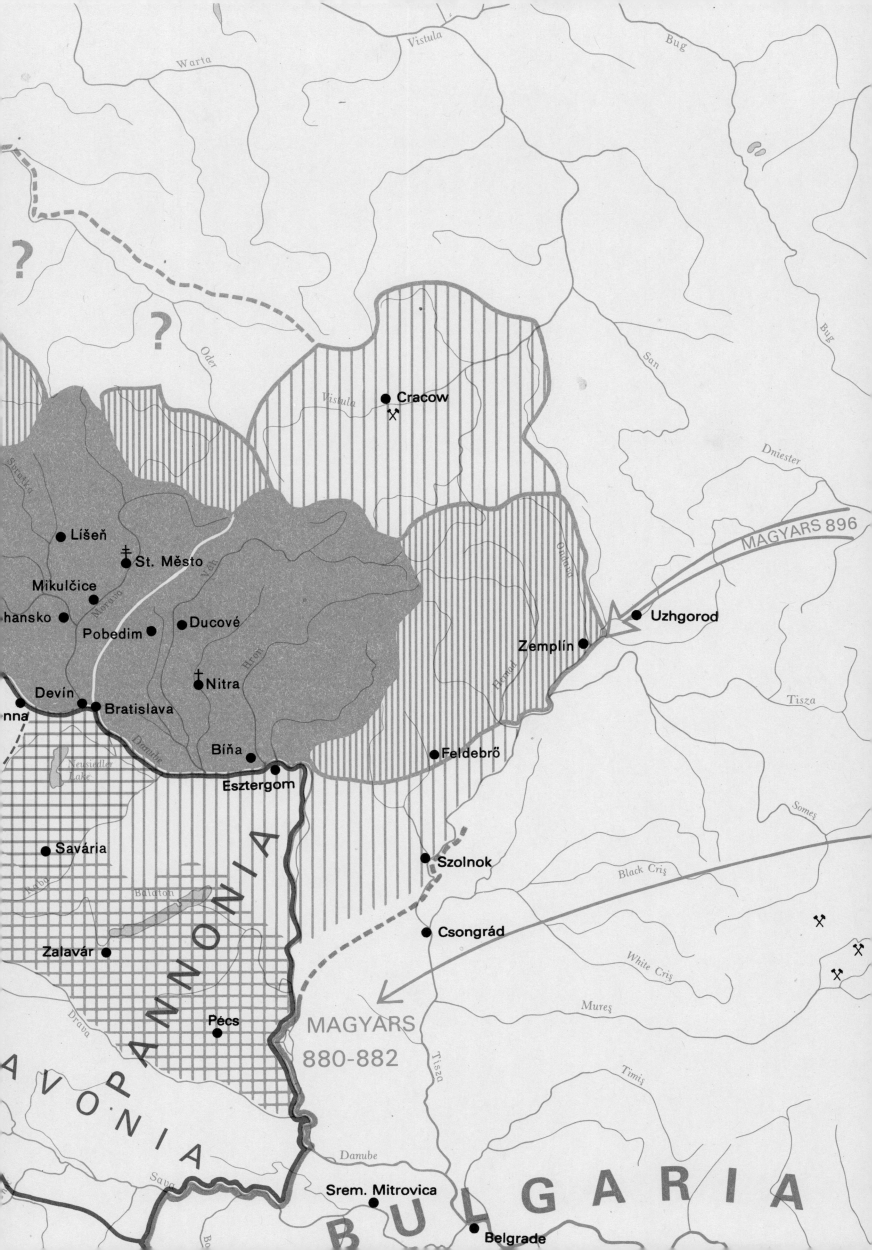

Warta

Vistula

Bug

?

?

Oder

Vistula

● Cracow ⚒

Bug

San

Dniester

MAGYARS 896

Sbratka

● Líšeň

‡ St. Město

Ondava

● Mikulčice

Morava

Hron

Váh

…hansko ●

● Pobedim

● Ducové

● Uzhgorod

● Devín

‡ Nitra

Zemplín ●

…nna

● Bratislava

Danube

● Bíňa

Esztergom ●

Feldebrő ●

Hornad

Tisza

Neusiedler Lake

P A N N O N I A

● Savária

Hrpa

Balaton

● Szolnok

Black Criş

Someş

● Zalavár

● Csongrád

White Criş

⚒

Drava

MAGYARS 880-882

Tisza

Mureş

⚒

⚒

● Pécs

S L A V O N I A

Sava

Danube

Timiş

Srem. Mitrovica ●

B U L G A R I A

● Belgrade

27. *Set of cast bronze belt ornaments. The large belt-end has a traditional motif of an animal fight. The oblong ornaments have a griffin, the symbol of light, life, and good. Nové Zámky*

28. *Set of cast bronze belt ornaments. The large belt-end is decorated with stylized animals, their heads turned backwards. Nové Zámky*

29. *Cast bronze belt-end with a motif of moving animals. Prša*

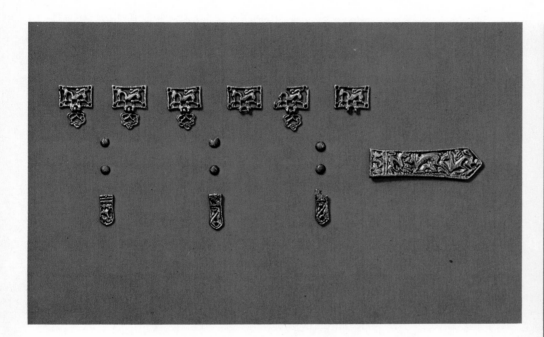

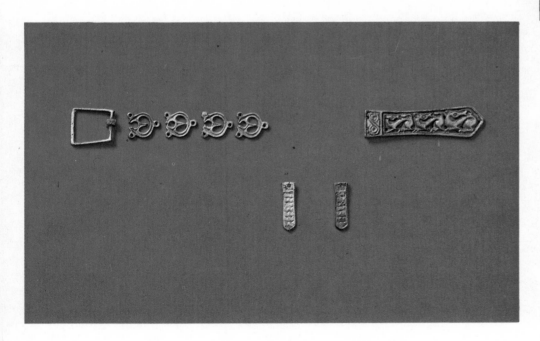

30. *Silver belt set. Nine oblong ornaments with an embossed animal motif. Six small belt-ends with an embossed motif. Belt-end with an embossed animal motif. Želovce*

31. *Cast bronze belt-end with a motif of resting griffins. Devínska Nová Ves.*

32. *Cast bronze belt-end with a motif of confronting griffins and a heart-shaped tendrillar pattern. Nové Zámky*

33. *Cast bronze oblong ornaments. Želovce*

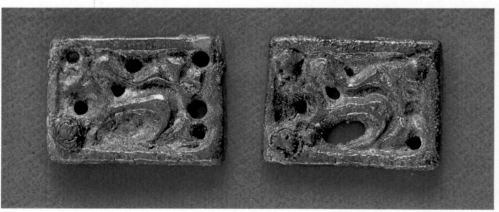

34. Cast bronze belt-end with a motif of confronting griffins. Nové Zámky

35.—37. Large cast bronze belt-end. On the obverse a bizarrely designed animal fight, on the reverse a circular tendrillar pattern. Šebastovce

38. *Two bronze trapezium-shaped buckles. Four cast bronze circular ornaments. Openwork phalera with the popular motif of a zoomorphic swastika. Žitavská Tôň*

39. *Set of openwork bronze phaleras with a spiral pattern. Devínska Nová Ves*

40. Cast bronze loop. Bernolákovo

41. Bronze ornament in the likeness of
a snake. Devínska Nová Ves

42. *Openwork bronze belt-end with a tendrillar vine pattern. Štúrovo*

43. *Gilded bronze ornament with a stylized plant pattern. Štúrovo*

44. *Cast bronze belt-end with a stylized tendrillar pattern. Devínska Nová Ves*

46. *Set of silver-plated bronze belt orna-*
    ments with a flat scroll pattern.
    Holiare

47. *Bronze belt-end with a lily design.*
    Žitavská Tôň

48. *Cast bronze belt-end with an openwork*
    checkered design. Želovce

49. *Cast bronze belt-end with an openwork*
    criss-cross pattern. Bernolákovo

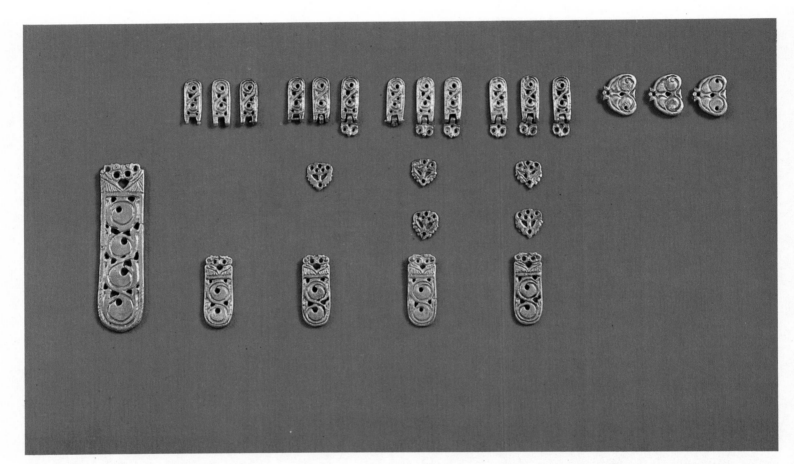

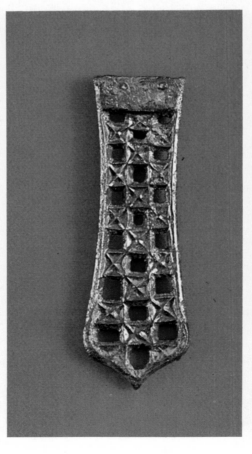

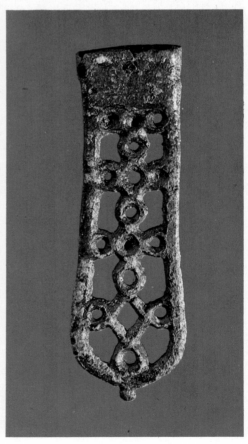

51. *Set of cast silver-plated belt ornaments. The disc-shaped ornaments with hinged rings are decorated with a stylized griffin. Large belt-end with a tendrillar motif. Small belt-end with an openwork frame. Small belt-end with plant ornamentation. Šaľa*

52. *Set of cast bronze belt ornaments with openwork latticing. Large belt-end, small belt-ends. Tongue-shaped ornaments with semicircular appendages and buckle. Nové Zámky*

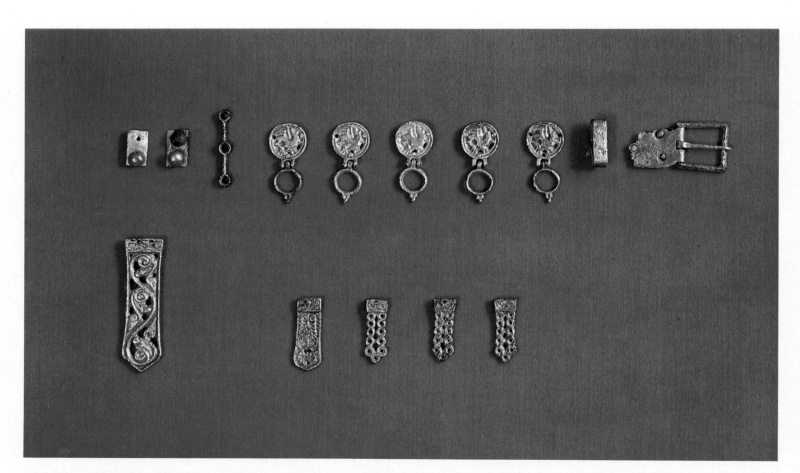

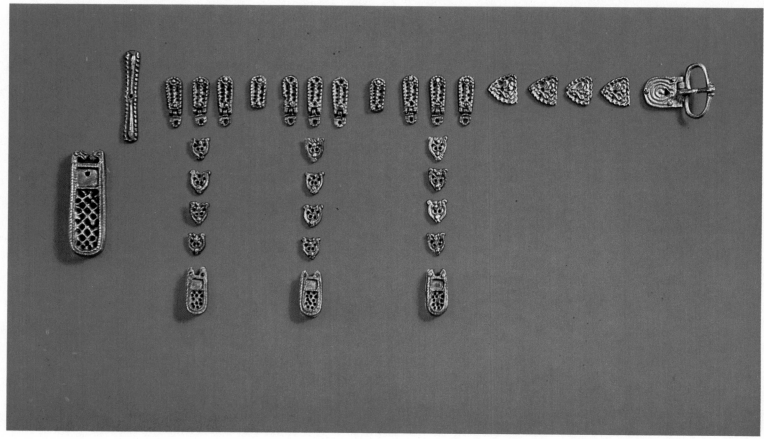

53. *Cast bronze hinge plate of a clasp with a peacock motif. Bronze belt-end with the motif of a stylized dragon. Hranič-ná nad Hornádom*

54. *Collection of ornaments from an equestrian grave. Two phaleras with a gilded boss-like ornamentation. Cast bronze belt-end with a hinge plate, shaped like a horse's head. Two belt-ends in the shape of a boars's head. Bronze ornaments in the form of eagles'heads. Devínska Nová Ves*

57. *Gold plated iron phalera decorated with a geometric and plant pattern.* Žitavská Tôň

58. *Set of cast bronze belt ornaments. The disc-shaped ornaments portray a Nereid on a sea-horse. Large belt-end, small belt-ends, ornament with confronting animal heads, buckle. Hevlín*

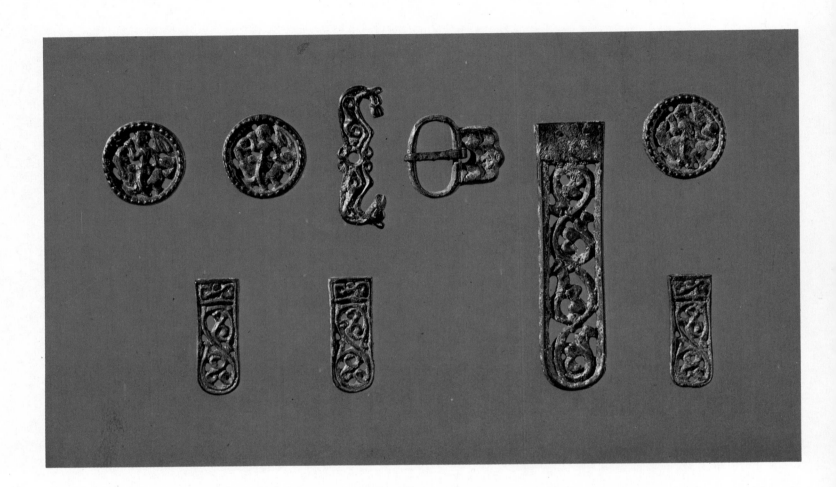

59. *Set of gilded bronze ornaments with stylized patterns of plants and scales. Bernolákovo*

60. *Gilded ornament with an openwork leafy pattern. Bernolákovo*

61. *Set of cast bronze belt ornaments. The anthropomorphic decoration of the large belt-end as well as the escutcheon-like ornaments with appendages indicate that this set dates from the second half of the 8th century. Nové Zámky*

62. *Large belt-end from plate 61. The crouching figure with the gesture of a suppliant is probably based on an oriental motif of an interceding spirit. Nové Zámky*

63. *Cast bronze belt-end with a figurative
    design of obscure significance. Šebas-
    tovce*

64. *Cast bronze belt loop with a figure of a gladiator, taken from a larger composition. Hraničná nad Hornádom*

65. Cast bronze belt-end with an openwork figurative pattern. The themes of the individual scenes are taken from the Hercules cycle. In the lower picture we see Hercules alone, with a club in his left hand and the skin of the Nemean lion in his right. In the center picture Hercules is killing the centaur Nessus; in the upper he is struggling with Hippolyte, the queen of the Amazons. The neck section of the belt-end depicts the wild boar killed by Hercules. The belt-end is a beautiful example of the revival of Hellenistic traditions. Dolné Dunajovice

66. *Cast bronze belt-end with the figure of a falconer. His costume is reminiscent of the Detva national costume of today. Moravský Ján*

67. *Bronze two-part clasp with a rose-pattern arrangement of colored stones. Holiare*

69. *Gold earrings with granulation and turquoise stones. Želovce*

70. *Gilded bronze earrings with pendants of granulated wreaths and blue beads. Holiare*

71. *Gold earrings with two-sided conical pendants with glass beads. Želovce*

72. *A selection of gold earrings. Želovce*

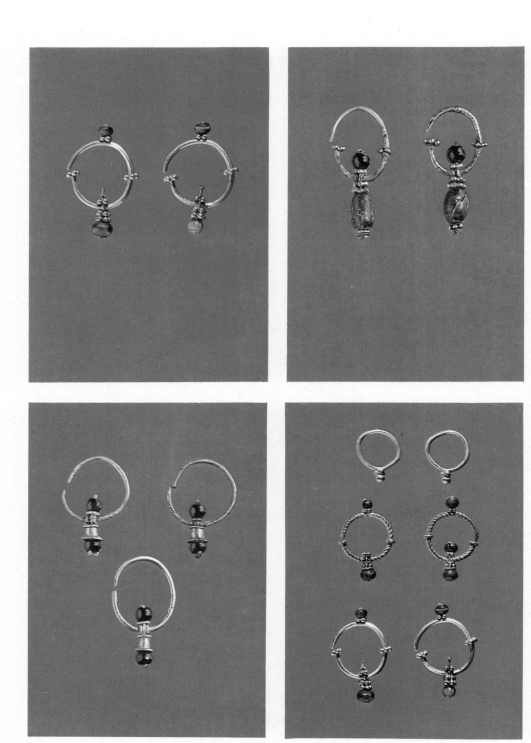

74. *Clay animal sculptures of ritual origin.*
    Mikulčice

76. *Examples of yellow pottery from Holiare and Nové Zámky*

77. *Yellow pottery from graves. A bottle-like vessel. A jug-like vessel with a broken handle. Nové Zámky*

The Cultural and Political Centers
of Great Moravia

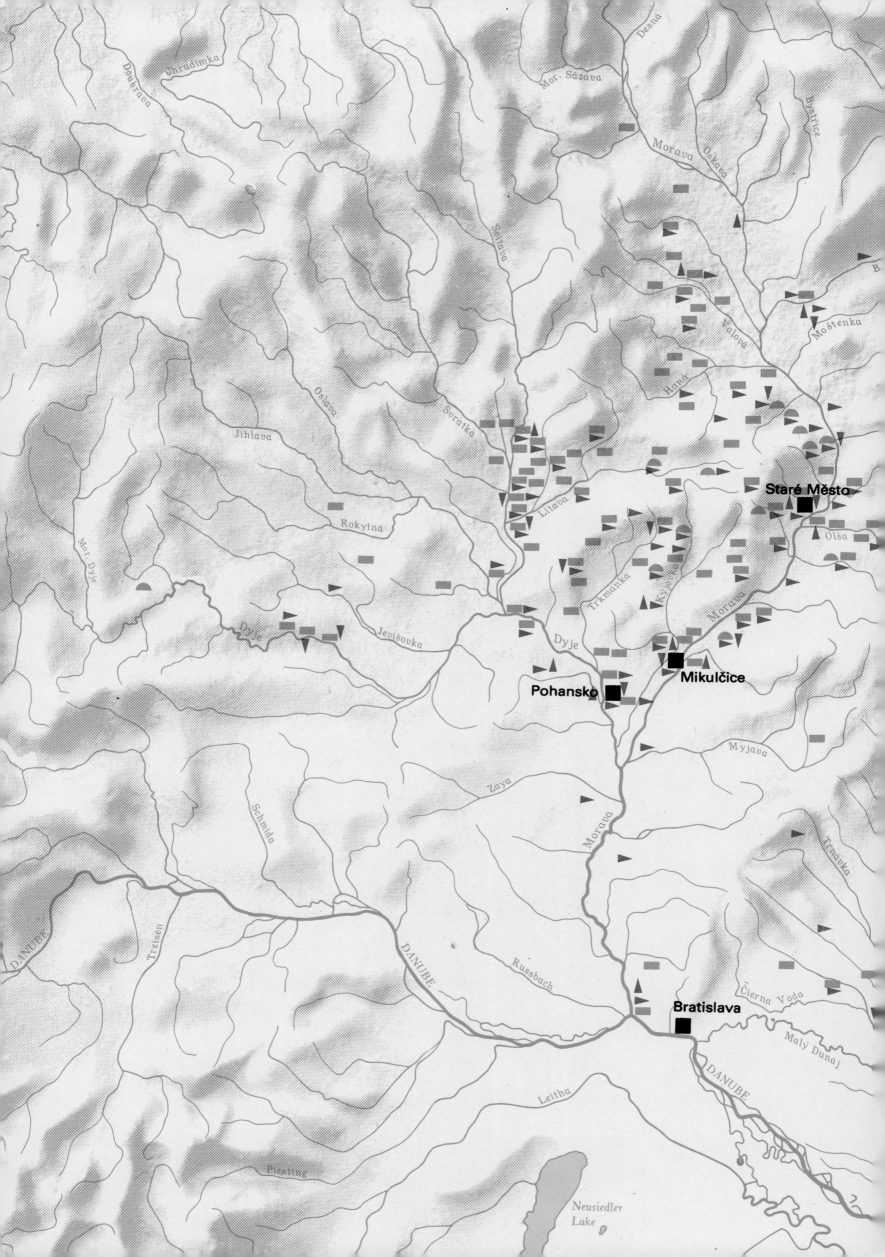

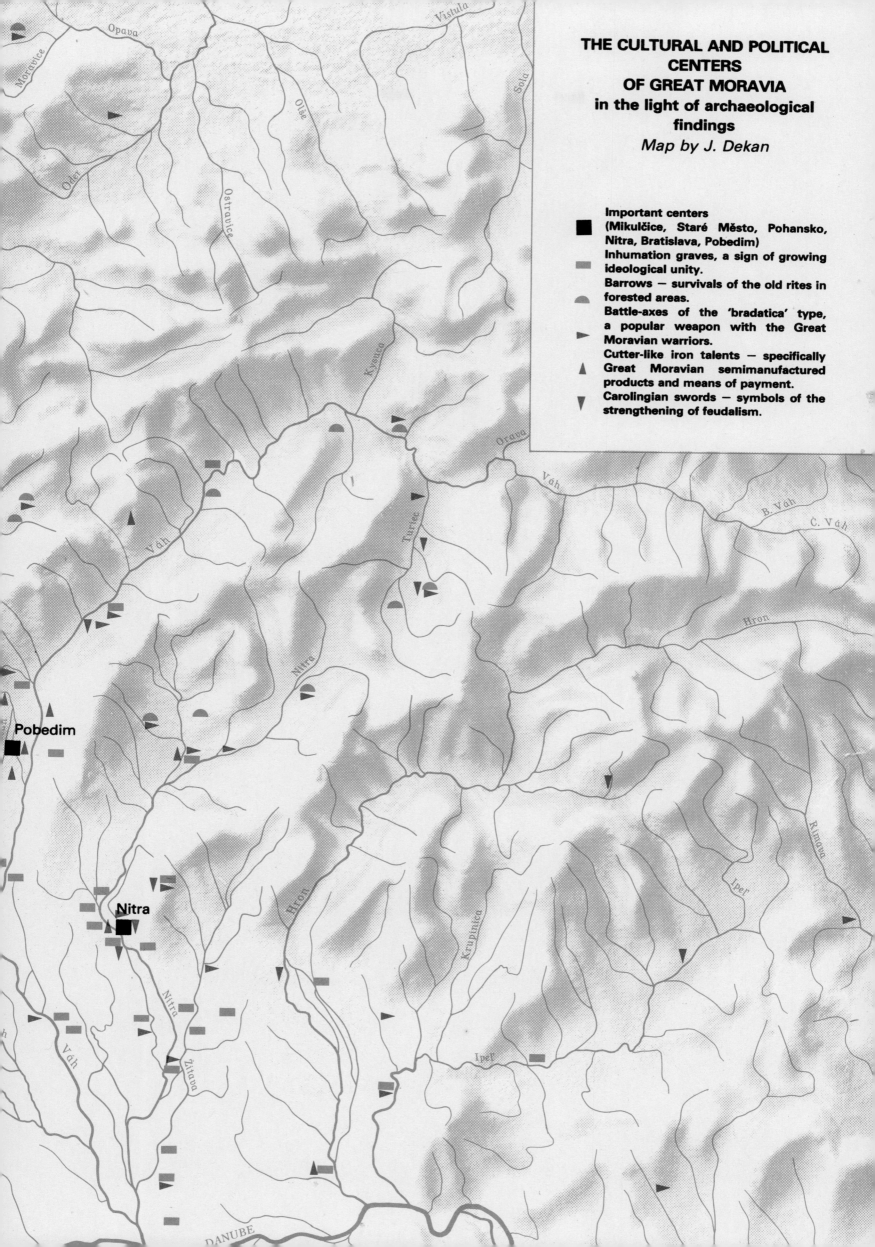

THE CULTURAL AND POLITICAL CENTERS OF GREAT MORAVIA
in the light of archaeological findings
Map by J. Dekan

Important centers
(Mikulčice, Staré Město, Pohansko, Nitra, Bratislava, Pobedim)

Inhumation graves, a sign of growing ideological unity.

Barrows — survivals of the old rites in forested areas.

Battle-axes of the 'bradatica' type, a popular weapon with the Great Moravian warriors.

Cutter-like iron talents — specifically Great Moravian semimanufactured products and means of payment.

Carolingian swords — symbols of the strengthening of feudalism.

Pobedim

Nitra

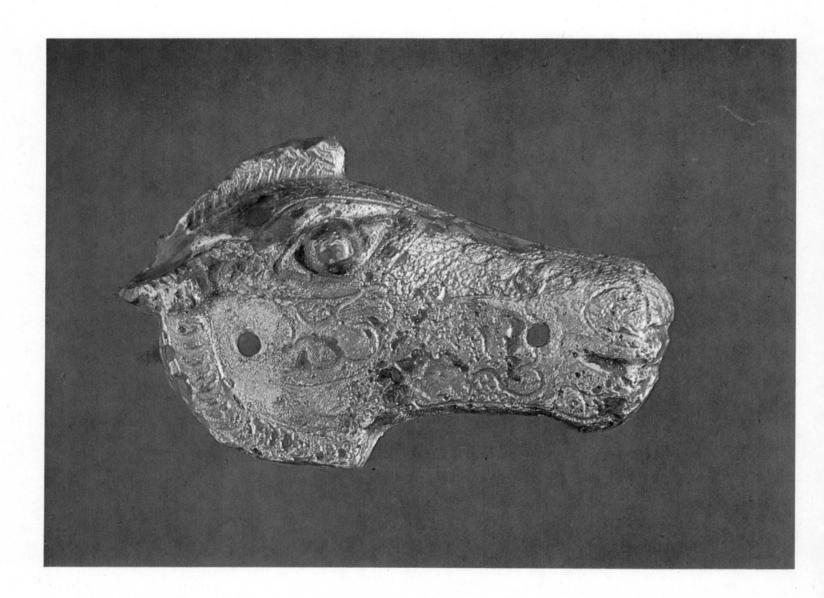

81. *Cast bronze ornament in the shape of a boar's head with an engraved semi-palmette design on a dotted background. Three small bronze ornaments of identical shape. Holiare*

82. *A selection of relics from the grave of a magnate. The gold plated escutcheon-shaped, trapezium-shaped and tongue-shaped ornaments belong to the last stage of development of the cast bronze industry of the middle Danubian region. The key-shaped lateral loop and cross-shaped ornament with other fragments were part of a horse's harness. Blatnica*

83. *Gilded bronze belt-end, whose technology and ornamentation place it at the beginning of the Blatnica horizon. Žitavská Tôň*

84. *Gilded disc-shaped ornaments from the same set. Žitavská Tôň*

85. *Cast bronze clasp with an openwork hinge plate. Šaľa*

86. *Cast bronze openwork belt-end. The stylized tree of life is an adaptation of an ancient Mediterranean symbol. Šaľa*

87. *Cast bronze rosette-shaped phalera. Gajary*

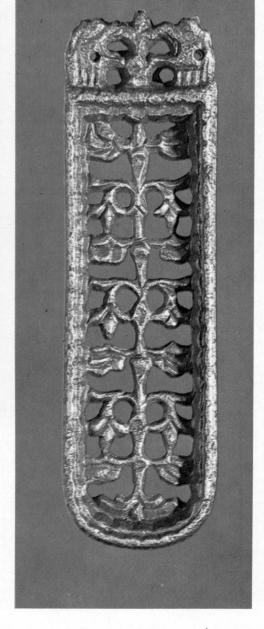

83	84	86
85		87

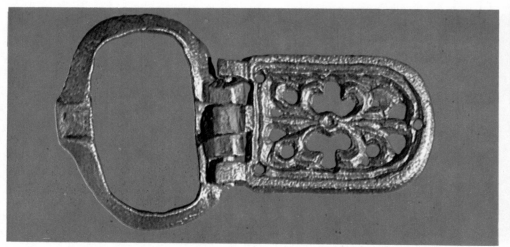

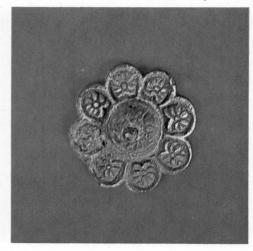

88. *Hilt of a nobleman's sword (see plate 82) decorated with gilded bronze and inlaid with silver. The emphatically geometric design combined with human masks points to Carolingian influence. Blatnica*

89. *Gilded cast bronze spurs with semipal-*
    mette and mask decoration on the sec-
    tioned arms. Mikulčice

90. *A set of gilded spurs with appurtenances. Strap end and buckle are decorated with the same semipalmette pattern. Mikulčice*

92. *Gilded bronze spurs with mask decoration, with appurtenances and gilded buttons. Mikulčice*

91. *Bronze spurs inlaid with silver and appurtenances. Mikulčice*

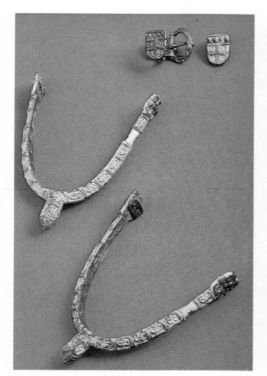

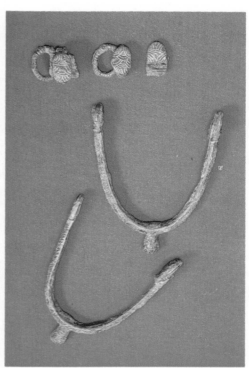

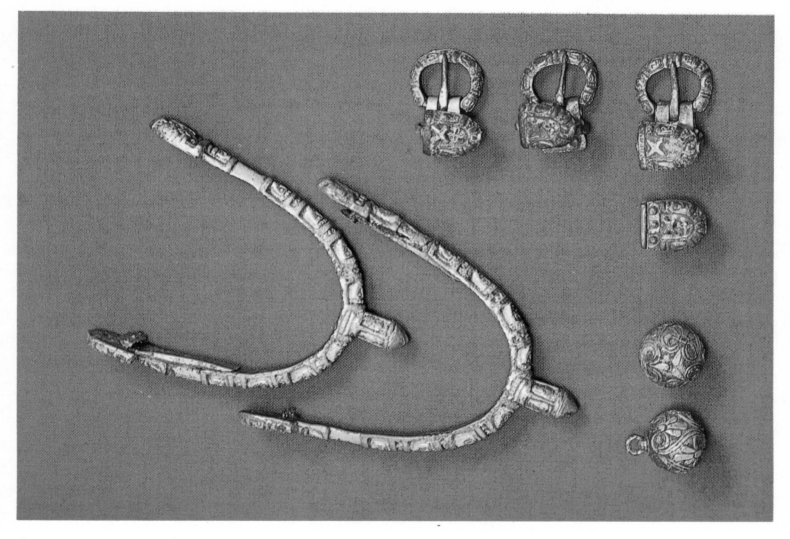

93. *Gilded bronze belt-end decorated with a notched pattern. Mikulčice*

94. *Gilded bronze belt-end with a motif of stylized snakes entwined in a heart-shaped pattern. Staré Město*

95. *Gilded bronze clasp in the shape of birds. Gilded bronze embossed belt-end. Mikulčice*

96. *Gilded bronze belt-end with a rich openwork plant pattern. Mikulčice*

98. *Two gilded bronze cast belt-ends with*
    openwork plant ornamentation. Two
    gilded heart-shaped ornaments. Two
    gilded ornaments with appendages.
    Gilded bronze ornament made up of
    six masks. Three gilded bronze triple-
    mask ornaments. Žitavská Tôň

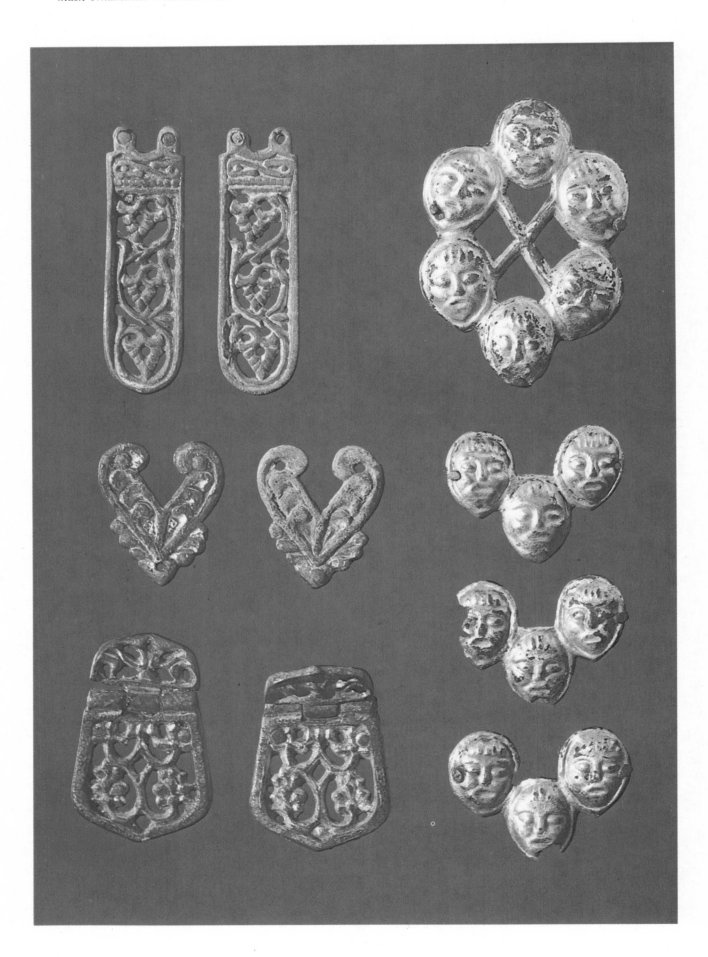

99. *Detail of six-mask phalera made of heavily gilded bronze. Žitavská Tôň*

101. *Fragment of a gilded silver belt-end. Confronting peacocks on either side of a stylized tree of life, in a medallion frame. The ribbons round the peacocks' necks point to Iranian influence. Mikulčice*

106. *Parts of a horse's harness, made of iron, with a markedly divided relief decoration. Size of the cross-shaped ornament. Pobedim*

106. Parts of a horse's harness, made of
iron, with a markedly divided relief
decoration. Size of the cross-shaped
ornament. Pobedim

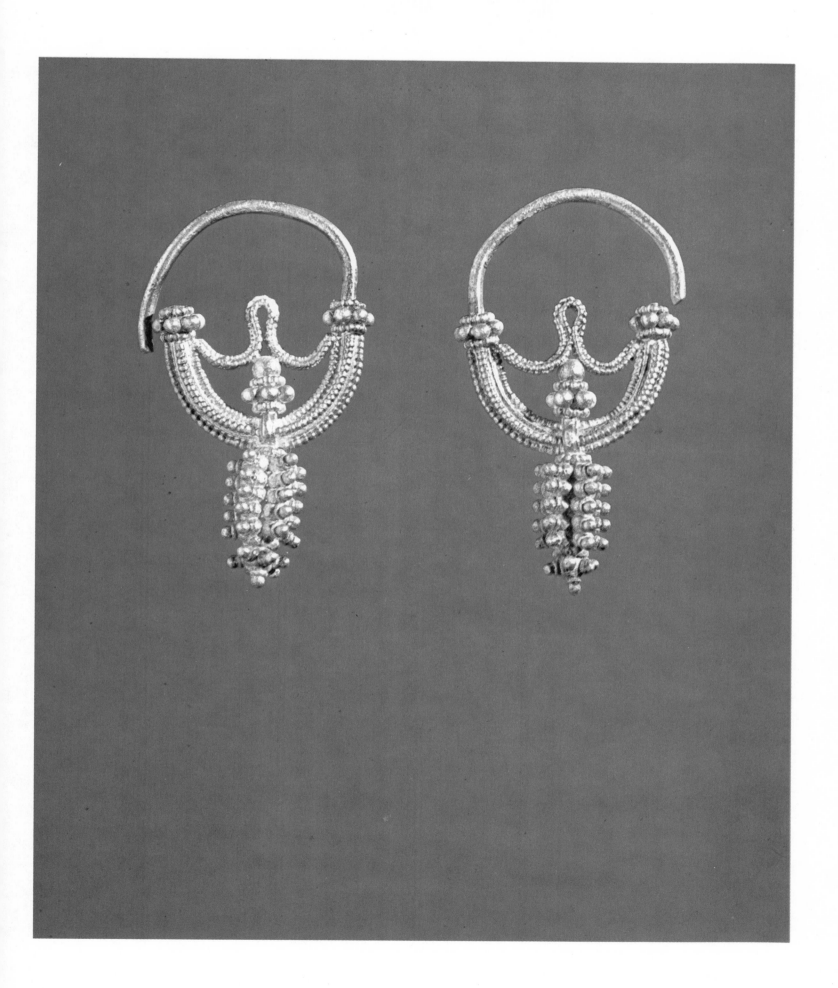

108. Antler 'salt cellar' decorated with an
engraved geometrical pattern. Pobedim

109. *Fragment of an antler hilt with a screw design. Mikulčice*
Bone whistle with an engraved geometrical pattern. Staré Město
Bone awl with a simple lattice design. Nitra, Martinský vrch

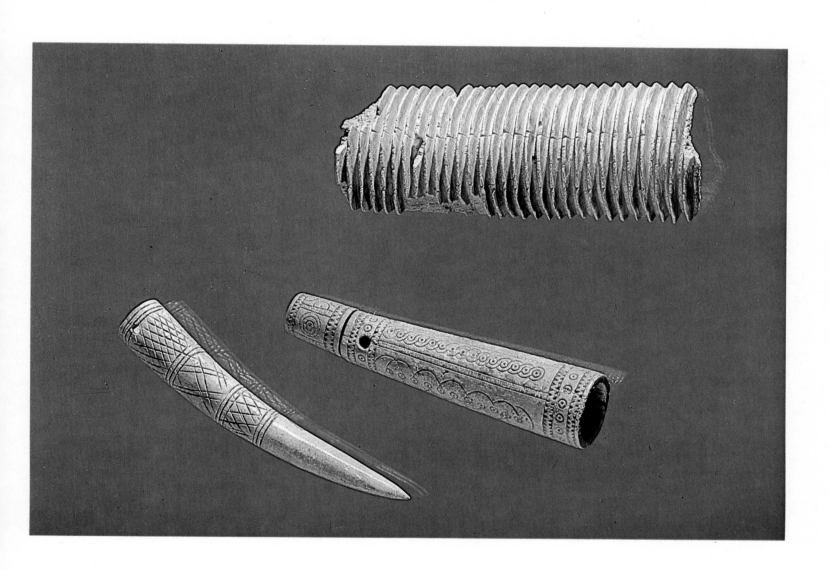

Moravia in the Present World

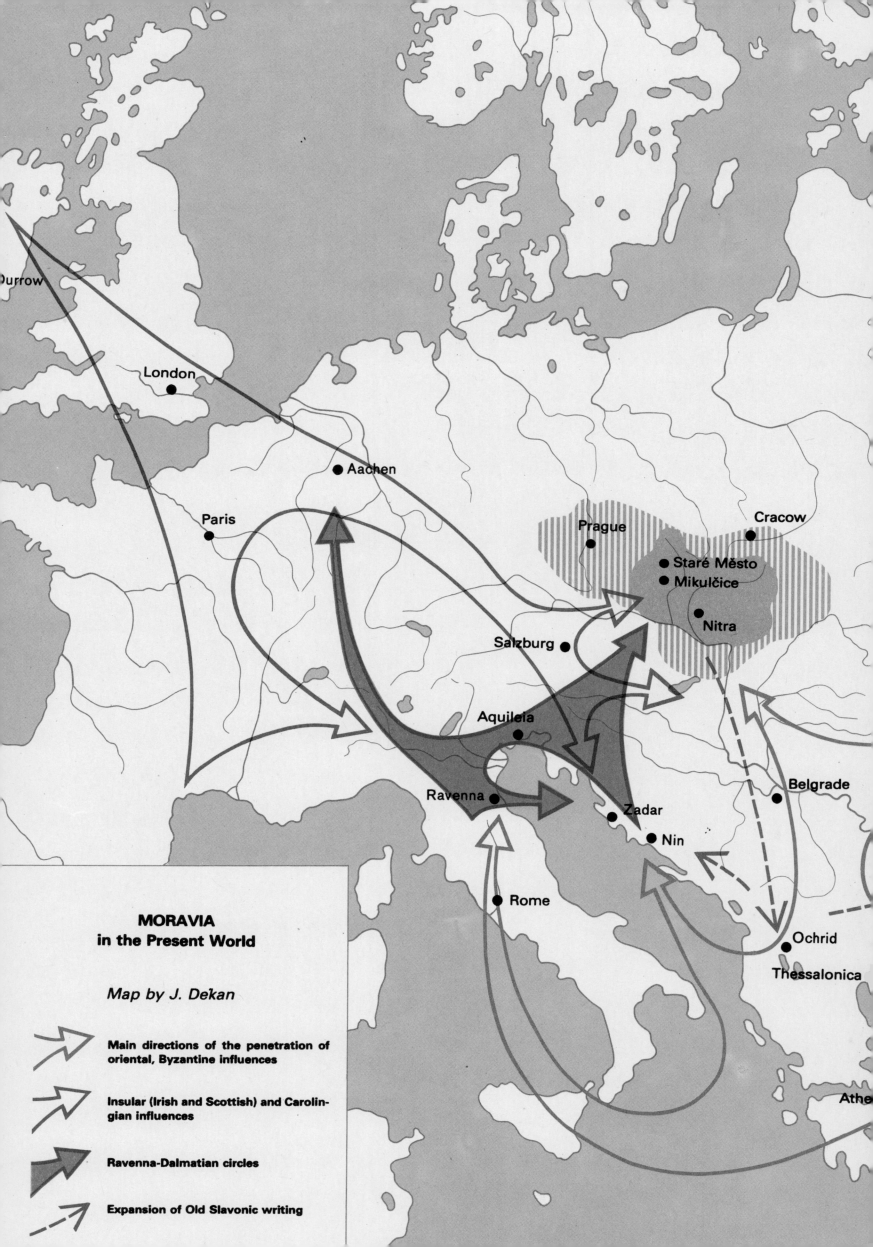

Durrow

London

Aachen

Paris

Prague

Cracow

Staré Město

Mikulčice

Nitra

Salzburg

Aquileia

Ravenna

Zadar

Belgrade

Nin

Rome

Ochrid

Thessalonica

Athe

**MORAVIA
in the Present World**

Map by J. Dekan

Main directions of the penetration of
oriental, Byzantine influences

Insular (Irish and Scottish) and Carolingian influences

Ravenna-Dalmatian circles

Expansion of Old Slavonic writing

Kiev

Cherson

Constantinople

Ephessus

Edessa

Antioch

Baghdad

111. *Gilded silver belt-end. Its wide, rounded frame is decorated with elements
formed from chain filigree. The central
design is a mirror-picture of a branching pattern. Mikulčice*

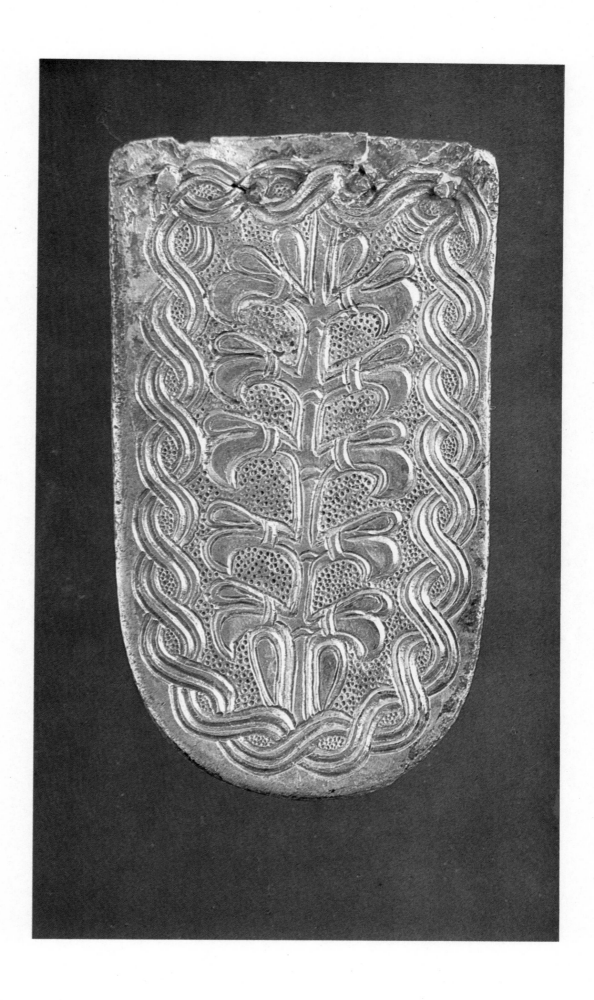

115. *Obverse of belt-end (plate 116) with a striking palmette design. Staré Město*

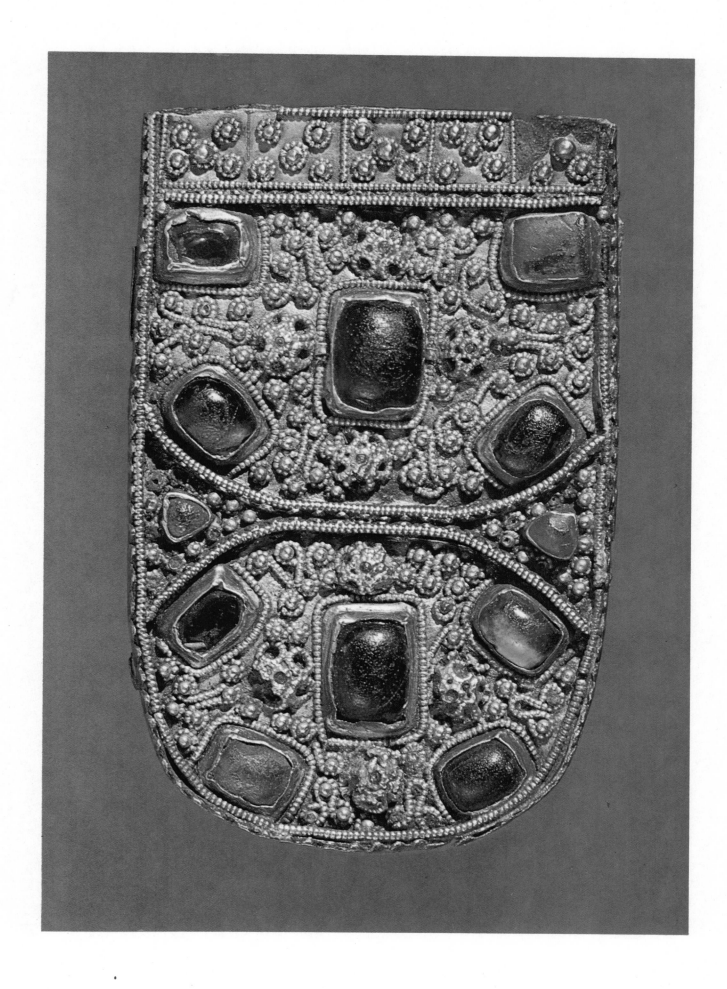

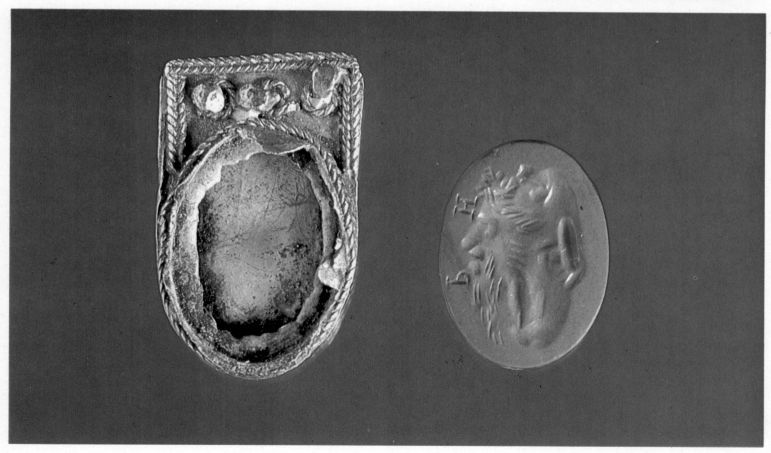

121. *Gilded bronze cross with the figure of Christ the Suppliant, with the symbols of the sun and moon on the transverse arms and an omega below. Mikulčice*

122. *Bronze two-part reliquary. Trnovec nad Váhom*

123. *Gilded bronze cross with masks. Mikulčice*

124. *Lead cross. Mikulčice*

126. *Cast silver cross with a crucified Christ. Mikulčice*

126. Cast silver cross with a crucified
     Christ. Mikulčice

128.—129. *Double surfaced gold buttons decorated with filigree and latticework. Mikulčice*

130. *Lantern-shaped gold buttons with colored glass stones. Mikulčice*

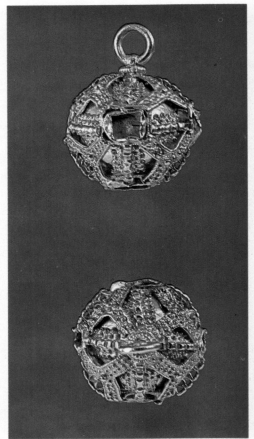

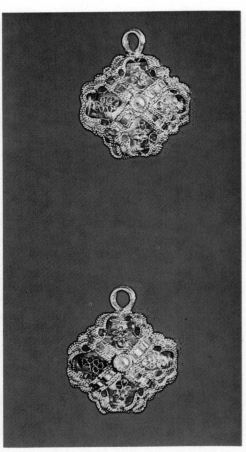

132.—33. *Antler discs with designs of an*
animal fight and a kneeling archer in
bas-relief. Mikulčice

134. *Rosette and circular ornaments made from antlers. Mikulčice*

135. *Gilded bronze buttons of polygonal shape, from the 10th century. Nitra — Amphitheatre*

138. *Two-colored glass buttons. Staré Město*

Glass button in a silver plaited basket. Břeclav, Pohansko
Gold spherical button with granulated surface. Staré Město

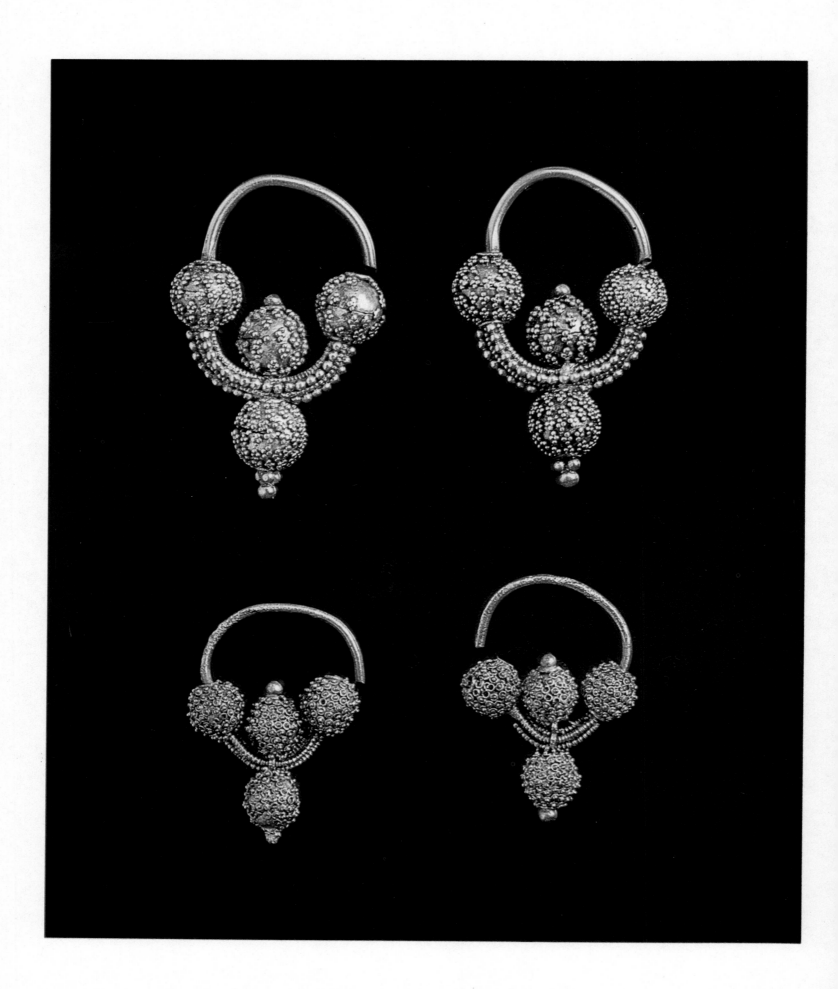

140. *Gold earrings with two-sided globular pendant and six globules on the ring. Silver globular earring with granulated wreath around the neck. Staré Město*

142. *Silver and gilded earrings with a column-shaped pendant finished at each end with a globule. Staré Město*

143. *Gold earrings with an exceptional number of granulated globules. Mikulčice*

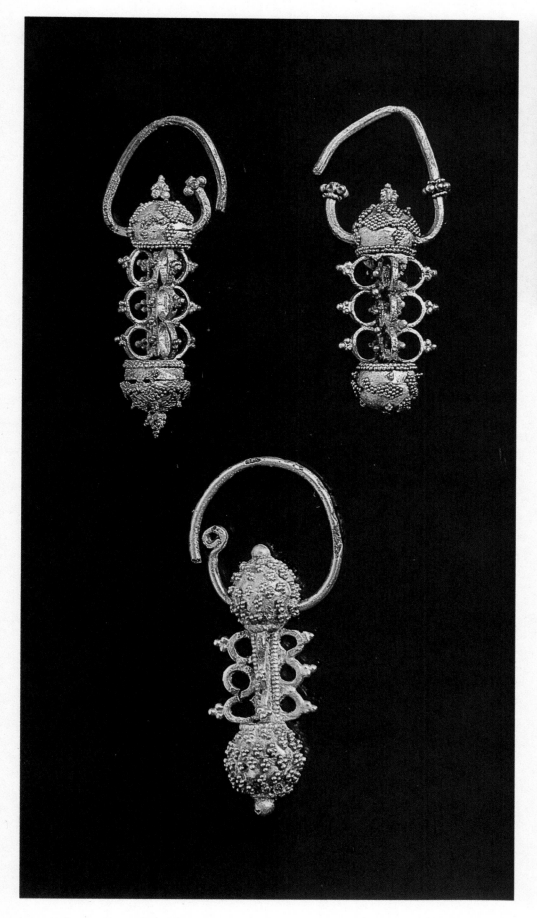

144. *Silver basket-shaped earrings with filigree — the final phase of the Great
Moravian traditions. Ducové*

146. *Silver basket-shaped earring. Trnovec nad Váhom*

147. *Silver earring with filigree baskets and a centrally set stone. Staré Město*

148. Selection of gold crescent-shaped earrings with granulated pendant. Upper and middle rows from Staré Město, below Brno, Staré Zámky pri Líšni

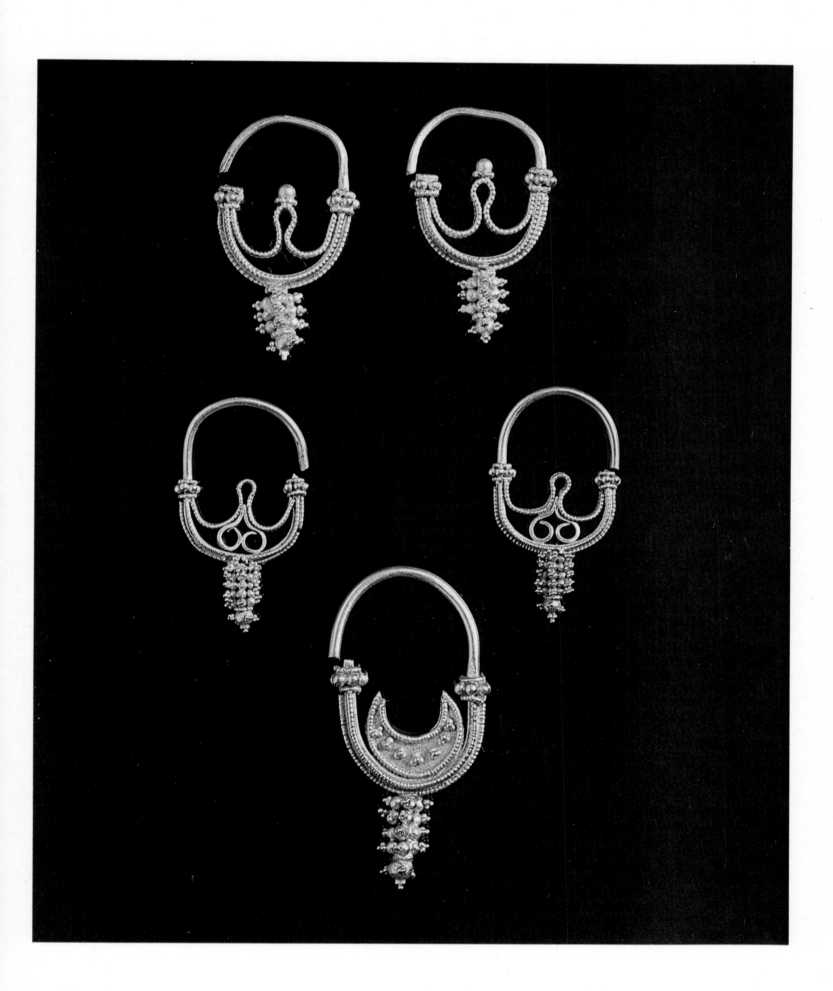

149. *Cast bronze crescent-shaped earring.*
     Nitra, Lupka

150.—151. *Cast bronze earrings of a vil-*
     lein. Nitra, Lupka

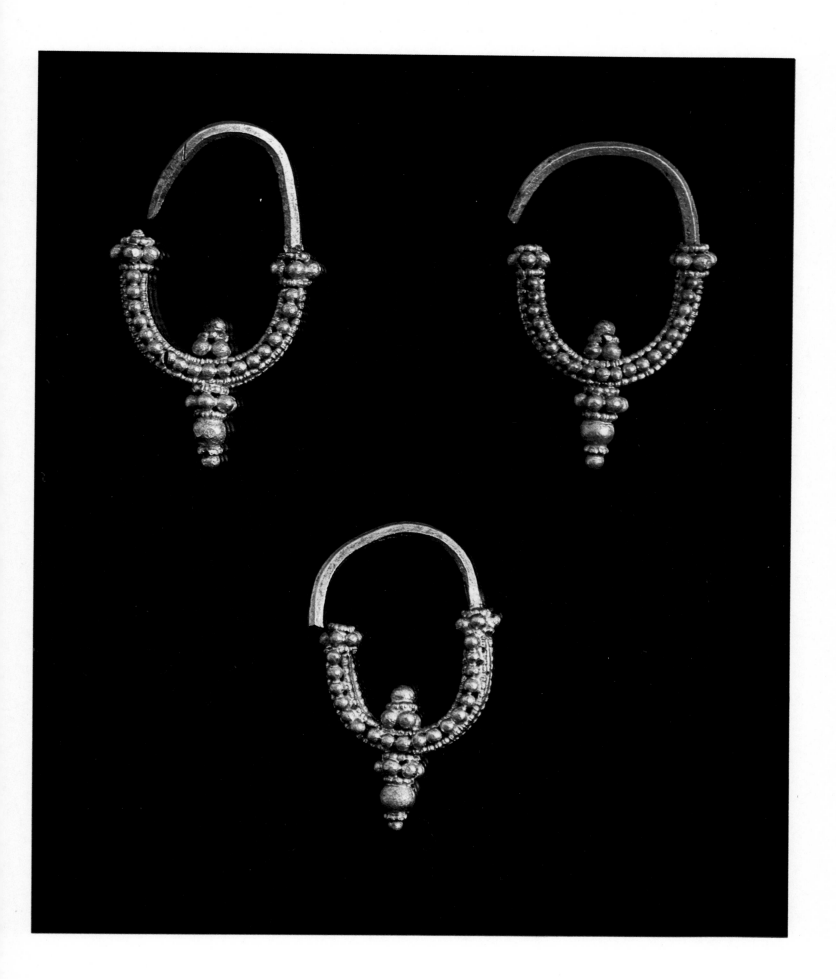

152. *Three silver earrings with granulated lower arcs and two-sided grape-like pendants. Staré Město*

153. Necklace of glass beads with a cast bronze lunular pendant. Dolní Věstonice

155. *Necklace with paste beads and a bronze
     lunar pendant. Nitra, Lupka*

156. *Cast bronze lunar pendant with its
     points turned inward. Nitra, Lupka*

157. *Silver lunar pendant with fine granulation on its geometrically divided surface. Staré Město*

158. *Gold lunar pendant, its edge decorated with chain filigree and center with granulated triangles and rhombuses. Mikulčice*

159. *Pendant from the necklace (plate 155). Nitra, Lupka*

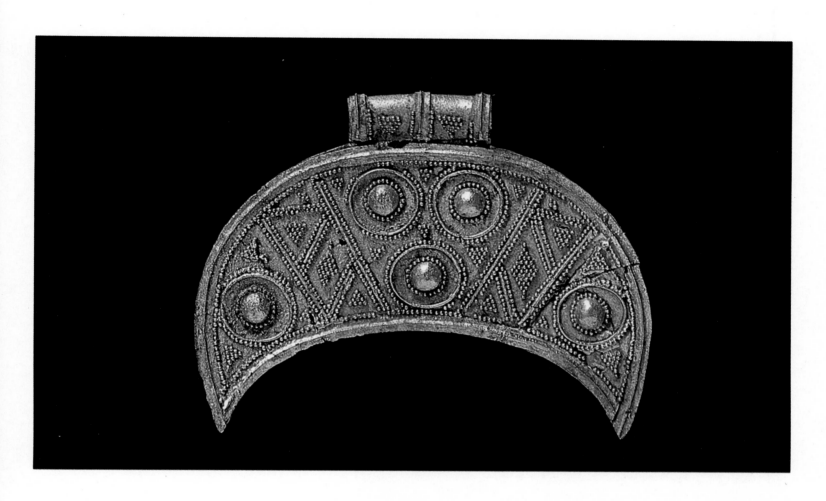

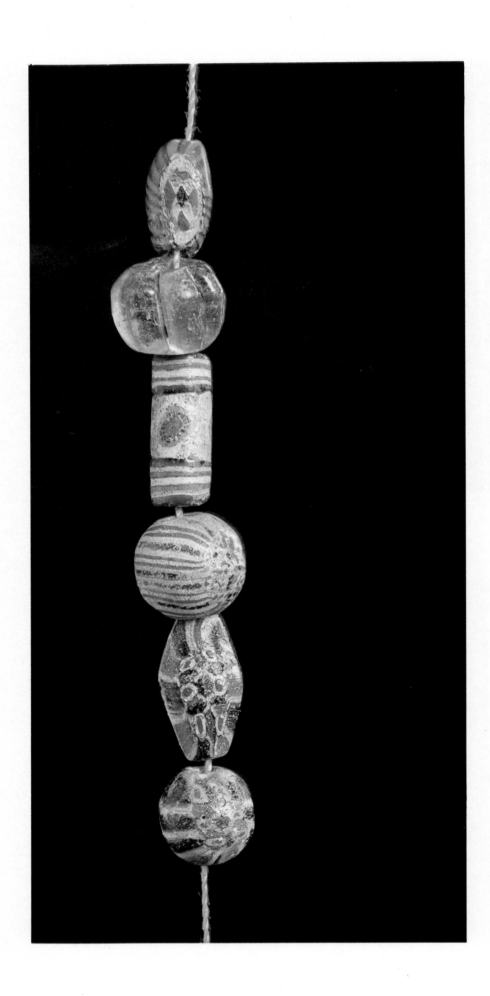

162. *Silver ring with a stone and granula-*
    tion. Mikulčice

163. *Silver ring with granulation, filigree*
    and blue stones. Mikulčice

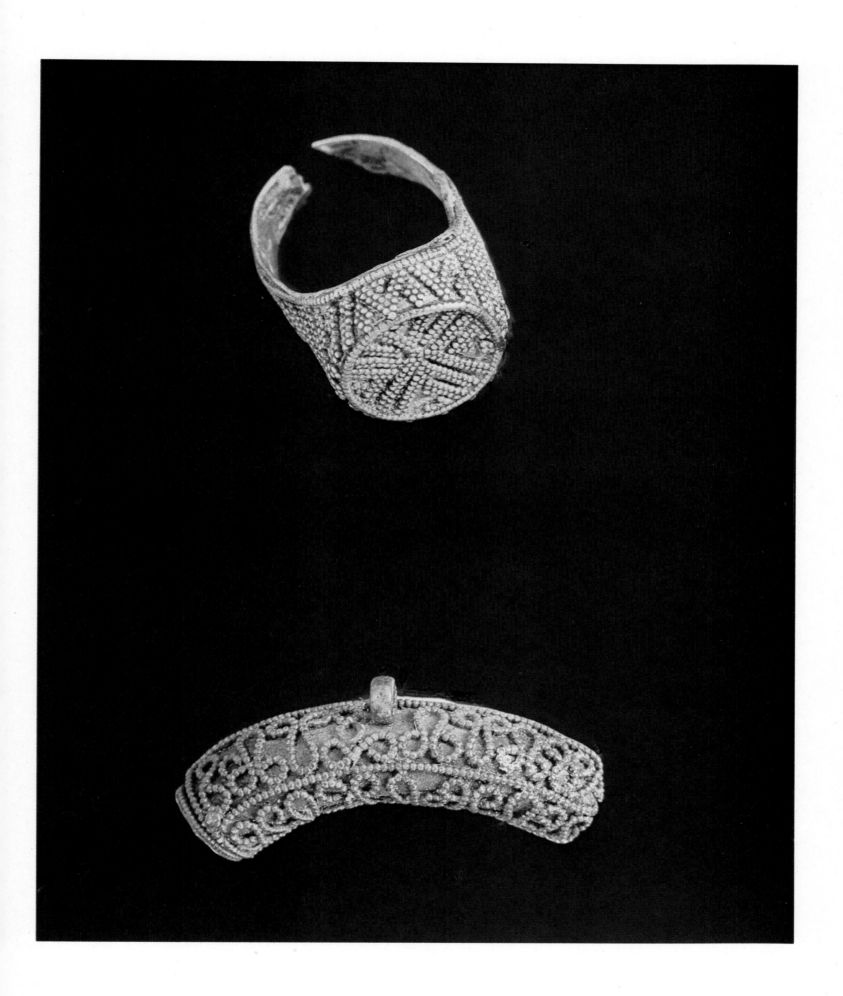

165. *Ritual twin vessel of smooth clay. Staré
Město*

164. Gilded silver ring with granulation. Silver cylinder-shaped reliquary decorated with filigree. Staré Město

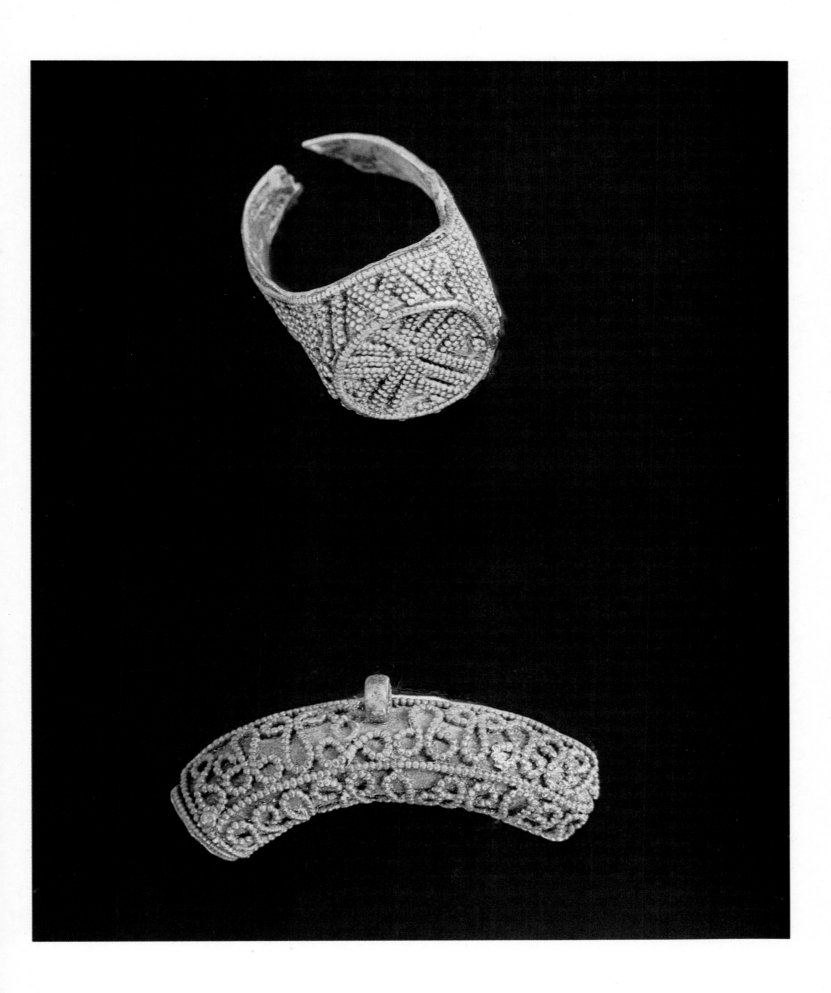

165. *Ritual twin vessel of smooth clay. Staré
    Město*

166. *Disc-shaped gilded bronze clasp. Staré Město*

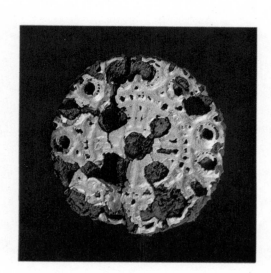

169. *Bronze and silvered semicircular cylindrical amulets decorated with filigree
and granulation. Stará Kouřim*

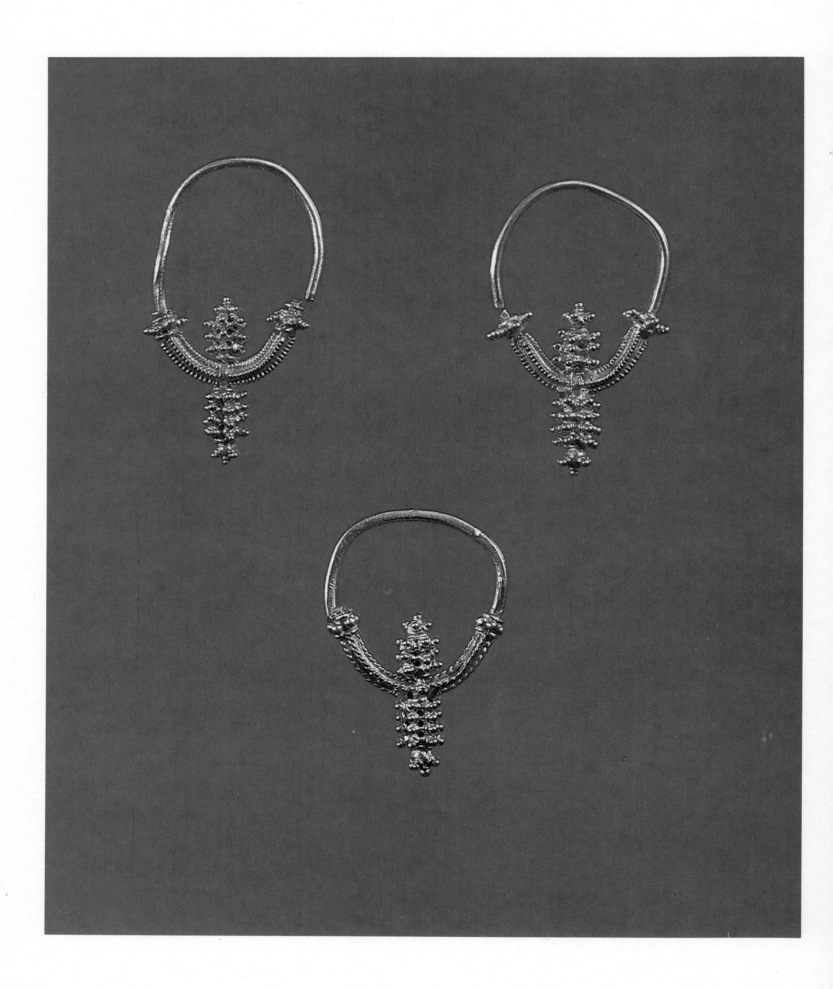

172. *Necklace with glass beads covered with gold foil, amethyst beads, and silver filigree baskets — a clear example of the dying out of Great Moravian traditions in the early feudal Hungarian kingdom. Ducové*

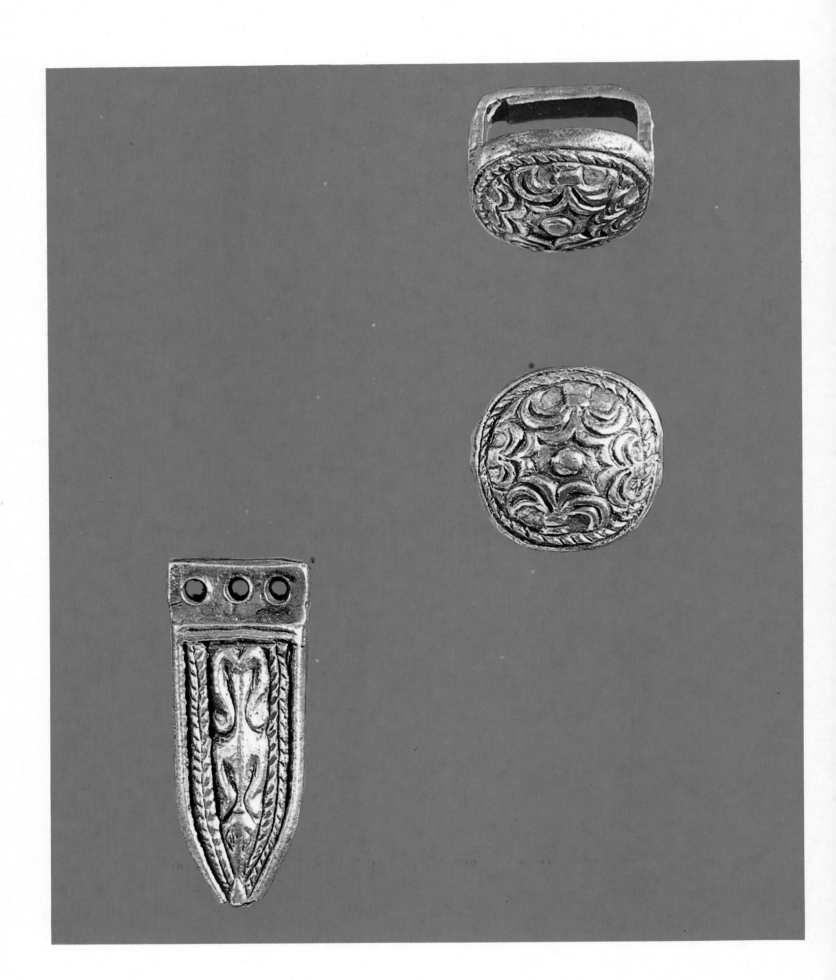

173. *Gilded silver belt-end with loops.*
  Kolín

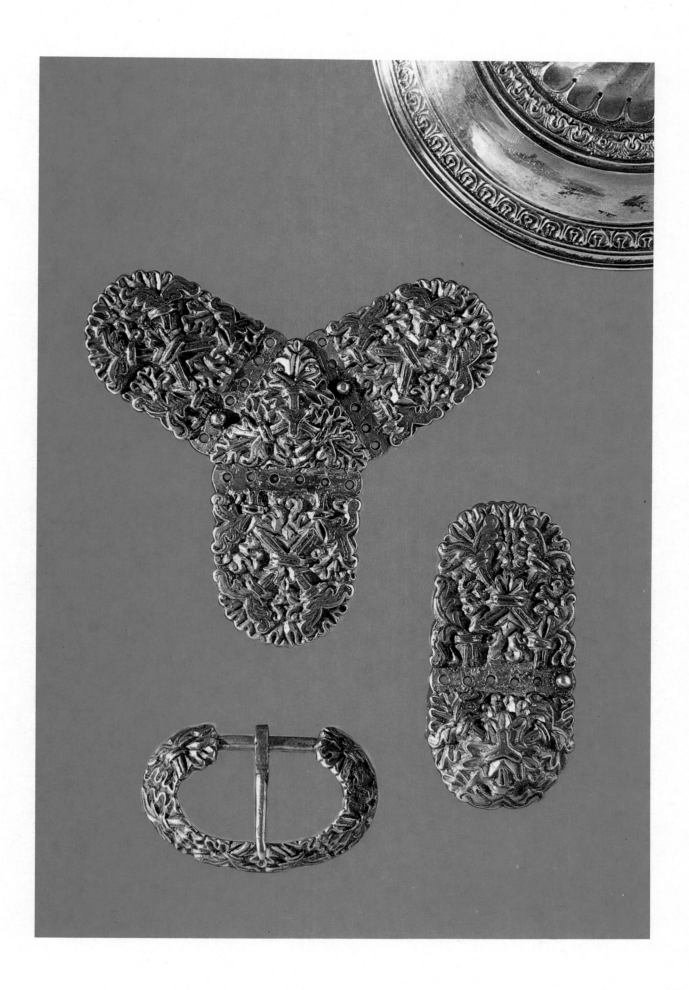

179. *Foundations of a church. Pohansko,*
       Břeclav

180. *Foundations of the triple-aisle basilica.*
       Mikulčice

181. *Foundations of a mausoleum. Mikul-*
čice

182. *Foundations of a complex of church*
buildings. Sady, Uherské Hradiště

183. *Foundation of a rotunda with two apses. Mikulčice*

184. *Foundations of a church with a square apse and supporting pillars. Mikulčice*

185. *Foundations of residential buildings on a magnate's estate. Pohansko, Břeclav*

186. *Foundations of a rotunda. Ducové, Moravany*

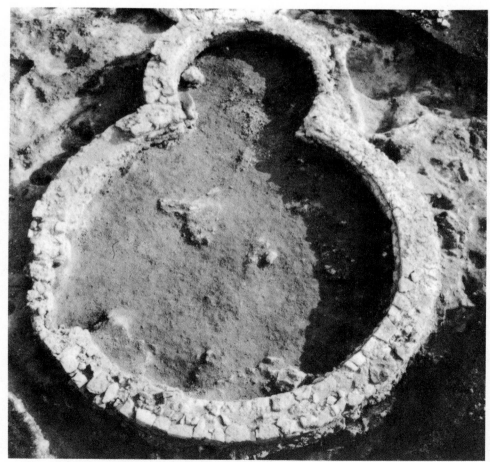

450/550   The great Slavic migration.

623   The first records of Samo's empire.

631   The Slavs won a victory over the Frankish army of King Dagobert near Vogastisburg.

658   King Samo died.

803   Slav princes recorded to be in the regions neighboring on Pannonia.

811   Mention made of Slav military commanders in the middle Danube region.

822   Moravian envoys visited Emperor Ludwig the Religious in Frankfurt.

830   The Salzburg archbishop Adalram consecrated the church at the court of Duke Pribina in Nitra. Mojmír then expelled Pribina from Nitra and formed a common state of Moravians and Slavs.

845   Fourteen Czech magnates were christened at Regensburg.

846   The East Frankish king, Ludwig the German, attempted to conquer Moravia and helped Rastislav to power.

847   Pribina became prince of the Balaton region.

852   Moravians granted asylum to the Frankish magnate Albgis.

855   Moravians repelled the attack of Ludwig the German and while in pursuit of him laid waste the territory of East Mark, south of the Danube.

857   Rastislav granted asylum to Prince Slaviteg, who had been driven out of Bohemia by the Franks.

860   Rastislav made an alliance with Karolman, governor of East Mark.

861   Pribina fell in a battle with the Moravians and was succeeded by his son Koceľ.

861/62   A Moravian mission, requesting ecclesiastical and legal independence from the East Frankish Empire, did not meet with success at the Curia Romana.

862   The Hungarians first appeared in the Carpathian basin.

863/64   In Byzantium the Moravian request was granted for a mission to be sent, which was led by Constantinus Philosophos and his brother, Methodius, who laid the foundations of writing in the Old Slavonic language and the Glagolithic script.

864   Rastislav was besieged by Ludwig the German at Devin and made a peace treaty with him.

865   Count Werinhar asked Rastislav for help against Ludwig the German.

866   Ludwig, son of Ludwig the German, requested alliance with Rastislav against his father.

867   The Byzantine mission left Moravia for the Balaton region, where it stayed for some time with Prince Koceľ, and from there went to Venice; at the end of the year it visited Rome at the invitation of the Curia.

868   The Byzantine mission acknowledged that the territory of Moravia belonged under the jurisdiction of the Curia Romana, which approved its operations in Moravia.

869 Constantinus Philosophos died (14 February); before his death he entered a monastery and adopted the name of Cyril (Kyril). The Curia sent Methodius to Rastislav, Svätopluk, and Kocel' and approved the use of Old Slavonic in the church services after a preceding Latin citation. Karlman pillaged Svätopluk's domain and Karol, the youngest son of Ludwig the German, was forced to retreat from Rastislav's stronghold.

The Curia appointed Methodius as the archbishop of Pannonia and Moravia.

870 Svätopluk surrendered to Karlman, captured Rastislav, and handed him over to the Franks.

Karlman ruled Moravia and seized the royal treasure. Methodius was captured, and Rastislav imprisoned and blinded in Regensburg.

871 Svätopluk was taken prisoner by Karlman, and Methodius was illegally imprisoned in Ellwangen.

The Moravians rose against Karlman and chose Slavomír as their prince; at the same time they banished all treacherous Frankish and Bavarian clergymen.

Karlman released Svätopluk, who joined with the Moravians and destroyed the Bavarian army near Rastislav's former seat.

872 The Moravians repelled the attacks of the Saxons, Thuringians, Franks, and Bavarians and won victory over their armies.

873 After the Moravian invasion of East Mark, Ludwig the German made a truce with them.

Archbishop Methodius was released from prison and he returned to Moravia.

874 Svätopluk's envoy made a peace agreement with Ludwig the German in Forchheim. In later years Svätopluk extended the boundaries of his empire. Great Moravia began to be formed.

880 At the request of Svätopluk, the Curia Romana took him and Great Moravia under its protection, regardless of all other temporal rulers. It permitted the use of the Old Slavonic liturgy in the church services after a preceding Latin citation.

Svätopluk ruled the territory of the Lusatian Sorbs and the Elbe region.

881 At the invitation of Emperor Bazil I, Methodius left for Constantinople, where his mission in Moravia was approved.

882 Svätopluk intervened in a dispute in East Mark and plundered part of its territory; in addition he repelled the attack of the Bulgarians in the Tisza valley, incited by Arnulf, Karlman's son. The Moravians asked Emperor Karl III in Worms for redress in the conflict with Arnulf.

883 Svätopluk pillaged Arnulf's domain in Pannonia.

884 Svätopluk laid waste Pannonia and annexed the Balaton region to his empire. Emperor Karl III made a peace treaty with Svätopluk and his princes at Monte Comiano.

885 Gorazd was chosen as Methodius' successor and a curse was laid on Wiching, the Bishop of Nitra.

Archbishop Methodius died on 6 February.

The Curia confirmed direct protection of King Svätopluk; it reestablished Wiching as Bishop of Nitra.

886 Legates of the Curia forbid Gorazd to carry out the function of archbishop and summoned him before the Curia; Wiching was entrusted with the administration of the Moravian church.

887 Two hundred eleven clergymen who used the Old Slavonic liturgy were banished from the Great Moravian Empire.

890 Arnulf negotiated with King Svätopluk at Omuntesberg and recognized Moravian sovereignty over the Bohemian tribes.

892 The Moravians waged war with Arnulf, who called on the Hungarians for help.

893 Wiching went over to Arnulf, who was defeated in Moravia.

894 King Svätopluk died and the Moravians made peace with the Bavarians.

895 The Bohemians left the Great Moravian Empire and submitted to Arnulf.

896 The Hungarians settled in the region beyond the Tisza.

897 The Lusatian Sorbs pledged tributes to Arnulf.

898 The younger son of King Svätopluk — Svätopluk II — with the help of Arnulf, rose against the elder son, Mojmír, and the Bavarians undertook two military expeditions into Moravia.

899 The Bavarian expedition released Svätopluk II from prison and escorted him to Bavaria.

The Moravians, as before, helped Count Isanrich to power in East Mark.

The legates of the Curia restored the Moravian archdiocese and consecrated one archbishop and three bishops for the territory of the Great Moravian Empire.

900 The Bavarians and Bohemians carried out a military invasion of Moravia.

901 The Moravians and the Bavarians made a peace agreement at Regensburg.

902 The Moravians defeated the Hungarians.

904/5 In Raffelstetten a customs tariff was imposed for trade in East Mark and with the neighboring Bohemians and Moravians.

907 The Hungarians defeated the Bavarians near Bratislava (4 July).

949/52 References to Great Moravia appear in the work of the Byzantine Emperor Constantine Porphyrogenetos.

950 The Old Hungarians occupied the south of Slovakia up to the Váh river.

973 Moravia became part of the Bohemian Empire of Boleslav II.

CATALOG OF PLATES

L = length, W = width, H = height, D = diameter

AÚ SAV = Archeologický ústav Slovenskej akadémie vied, Nitra (Archaeological Institute, Slovak Academy of Sciences, Nitra)

AÚ SNM= Archeologický ústav Slovenského národného múzea, Bratislava (Archaeological Institute, Slovak National Museum, Bratislava)

AÚ ČSAV= Archeologický ústav Československé akademie věd, Brno (Archaeological Institute, Czechoslovak Academy of Sciences, Brno)

VM= Východoslovenské múzeum, Košice (East Slovakian Museum, Košice)

OM= Okresní museum, Znojmo (District Museum, Znojmo)

MM= Městské museum, Brno (Municipal Museum, Brno)

NP= Národní památník, Mikulčice (National Monument, Mikulčice)

MNM= Magyar nemzeti múzeum, Budapest (Hungarian National Museum, Budapest)

M= Múzeum, Bojnice (Bojnice Museum)

OM= Okresní museum, Uherské Hradiště (District Museum, Uherské Hradiště)

NM= Národní museum, Praha (National Museum, Prague)

1. Silver belt-end with a hammered pattern in the form of interwoven figure eights (L 9.7 cm). Holiare. AÚ SAV

2. Silver and gold plated iron helmet of the Baldenheim type (H 19 cm, L 22.6 cm, W 21 cm). Dolné Semerovce. AÚ SNM

3. Gold-plated iron helmet of the Baldenheim type (H 12 cm, L 22.8 cm, W 17.7 cm). Dolné Semerovce. AÚ SNM

4.—6. Fragments of an ivory pyxis (H 7.2 cm). Žuráň. MM

7. Silver belt-end with an embossed zigzag pattern (L 6.2 cm). Holiare. AÚ SAV

8. Set of gilded belt ornaments with an embossed pattern and pale blue glass stones (L of the large belt-end, 7.6 cm; of the small belt-ends, 2.3 cm; edges of the square ornaments, 2.5 cm). Želovce. AÚ SAV

9. Set of gilded belt ornaments with embossed ornamentation and missing glass stones (L of the large belt-end, 7.2 cm; of the small belt-end, 2.6 cm; D of the rosette ornaments, 2.8 cm). Želovce. AÚ SAV

10. Silver earrings with globular pendants (H 5.2 cm and 4 cm). Želovce. AÚ SAV

11. Gold earrings with hollow pendants decorated with granulation (H 3.5 cm). Želovce. AÚ SAV

12. Silver earrings with globular pendants (H 4.6 cm). Želovce. AÚ SAV

13. Silver earrings with a hollow sphere set with dark blue stones; the neck of the pendant is surrounded by globules (H 5.4 cm). Holiare. AÚ SAV

14. Silver earring with unusual pendant (H 6 cm). Holiare. AÚ SAV

15. Silver earrings with a richly molded neck and a pearl-shaped pendant studded with gilded decorations (H 4.2 cm). Holiare. AÚ SAV

16. Bronze earrings with a crescent-shaped lower arc and globular ornamentation (H 4.8 cm). Želovce. AÚ SAV

17. Beaten silver crescent-shaped earrings with starlike pendants (H 4 cm). Želovce. AÚ SAV

18. Beaten silver crescent-shaped earring with a starlike pendant (H 7.5 cm). Holiare. AÚ SAV

19. Cast bronze crescent-shaped earrings with starlike pendants (H 3.4 cm). Štúrovo. AÚ SAV

20. Two square gold ornaments with a hammered design (L 3 cm, W 2.8 cm); gold two-part clasp set with dark blue oval stones (H 2.7 cm, W 2.3 cm). Želovce. AÚ SAV

21. Open silver bracelets (D 6.9 and 6.6 cm); silver ring with a dark blue stone in a silver setting (D 1.8 cm). Želovce. AÚ SAV

22. Gold earring with a cylindrical granulated pendant (H 2.8 cm). Želovce. AÚ SAV

23. Part of a silver treasure-trove: 1. silver hemispherical dish with embossed ornamentation (H 3.4 cm, D 16.4 cm); 2. silver chalice (H 7.4 cm, D 9.2 cm); 3. silver bracelet with hammered ornamentation (D 8.2 cm); 4. silver bracelet with hammered ornamentation (D 6 cm); 5. cast silver earring (H 3.9 cm). Zemiansky Vrbovok. AÚ SAV

24. Pottery of the Prague type. MM

25. Pottery of the Tisza type from inhumation graves (H 18 cm, 15 cm, 11 cm). Želovce. AÚ SAV

26. Hand-molded pottery from inhumation graves (H 18 cm, 15 cm, 13 cm). Želovce. AÚ SAV

27. Set of cast bronze belt ornaments. The large belt-end has a traditional motif of an animal fight (L 10.2 cm). The oblong ornaments have a griffin, the symbol of light, life, and good. Nové Zámky. AÚ SAV

28. Set of cast bronze belt ornaments. The large belt-end is decorated with stylized animals, their heads turned backwards (L 9.7 cm). Size of the eyelet ornaments 2 × 2.5 cm; length of the small belt-ends 3 cm. Nové Zámky. AÚ SAV

29. Cast bronze belt-end with a motif of moving animals (L 12.4 cm). Prša. AÚ SAV

30. Silver belt set. Nine oblong ornaments with an embossed animal motif (L 2.8 cm). Six small belt-ends with an embossed motif (L 2.8 cm). Belt-end with an embossed animal motif (D 5.6 cm). Želovce. AÚ SAV

31. Cast bronze belt-end with a motif of resting griffins (L 8.7 cm) Devínska Nová Ves. AÚ SNM

32. Cast bronze belt-end with a motif of confronting griffins and a heart-shaped tendrillar pattern (L 8.9 cm). Nové Zámky. AÚ SAV

33. Cast bronze oblong ornaments (L 3.7 cm). Želovce. AÚ SAV

34. Cast bronze belt-end with a motif of confronting griffins (L 8.5 cm). Nové Zámky. AÚ SAV

35.–37. Large cast bronze belt-end. On the obverse a bizarrely designed animal fight; on the reverse a circular tendrillar pattern (L 12.5 cm). Šebastovce. VM

38. Two bronze trapezium-shaped buckles (L 3.1 cm). Four cast bronze circular ornaments (D 2 cm). Openwork phalera with the popular motif of a zoomorphic swastika (D 6.1 cm). Žitavská Tôň. AÚ SNM

39. Set of openwork bronze phaleras with a spiral pattern (D 4.1 cm and 3.8 cm). Devínska Nová Ves. AÚ SNM

40. Cast bronze loop (H 3.2 cm, D 2.2 cm). Bernolákovo. AÚ SNM

41. Bronze ornament in the likeness of a snake (H 2.7 cm). Devínska Nová Ves. AÚ SNM

42. Openwork bronze belt-end with a tendrillar vine pattern (L 14.5 cm). Štúrovo. AÚ SAV

43. Gilded bronze ornament with a stylized plant pattern (L of edges 2.2 cm). Štúrovo. AÚ SAV

44. Cast bronze belt-end with a stylized tendrillar pattern (L 9.5 cm). Devínska Nová Ves. AÚ SNM

45. Gilded bronze belt-end decorated with a tendrillar motif (L 10.3 cm and 3.5 cm). Devínska Nová Ves. AÚ SNM

46. Set of silver-plated bronze belt ornaments with a flat scroll pattern (L of the large belt-end 9.4 cm). Holiare. AÚ SAV

47. Bronze belt-end with a lily design (L 3.2 cm). Žitavská Tôň. AÚ SNM

48. Cast bronze belt-end with an openwork checkered design (L 11.7 cm). Želovce. AÚ SNM

49. Cast bronze belt-end with an openwork criss-cross pattern (L 8 cm). Bernolákovo. AÚ SNM

50. Gilded cast bronze ornaments in the shape of stylized animal masks (W 2.4 cm). Žitavská Tôň. AÚ SNM

51. Set of cast silver-plated belt ornaments. The disc-shaped ornaments with hinged rings are decorated with a stylized griffin (H 4.8 cm, D 2.2 cm). Large belt-end with a ten-drillar motif (L 8.2 cm). Small belt-end with an openwork frame (L 3.9 cm). Small belt-end with plant ornamentation (L 4.4 cm). Šaľa. AÚ SNM

52. Set of cast bronze belt ornaments with openwork latticing. Large belt-end (L 7.1 cm). Small belt-ends (D 3 cm). Tongue-shaped ornaments with semi-circular appendages (L 3.6 cm). Nové Zámky. AÚ SNM

53. Cast bronze hinge plate of a clasp with a peacock motif (L 4.9 cm). Bronze belt-end with the motif of a stylized dragon (L 10.5 cm). Hraničná nad Hornádom. VM

54. Collection of ornaments from an equestrian grave. Two phaleras with a gilded boss-like ornamentation (D 9.1 cm). Cast bronze belt-end with a hinge plate, shaped like a horse's head (L 6.9 cm). Two belt-ends in the shape of a boar's head (L 3.9 cm). Bronze ornaments in the form of eagles' heads (L 4.4 cm). Devínska Nová Ves. AÚ SNM

55. Detail of the belt-end in the shape of a horse's head (plate 54). Devínska Nová Ves. AÚ SNM

56. Gold-plated iron phalera (D 13.5 cm). Devínska Nová Ves. AÚ SNM

57. Gold-plated iron phalera decorated with a geometric and plant pattern. Žitavská Tôň. AÚ SNM

58. Set of cast bronze belt ornaments. The disc-shaped ornaments portray a Nereid on a sea-horse (D 2.5 cm). Large belt-end (L 6.2 cm). Small belt-ends (L 3.6 cm). Ornament with confronting animal heads (L 4.3 cm). Hevlín. OM Znojmo

59. Set of gilded bronze ornaments with stylized patterns of plants and scales. Bernolákovo. AÚ SNM

60. Gilded ornament with an openwork leafy pattern (L 4 cm). Bernolákovo. AÚ SNM

61. Set of cast bronze belt ornaments. The anthropomorphic decoration of the large belt-end (L 14 cm) as well as the escutcheon-like ornaments with appendages (H 5 cm) indicate that this set dates from the second half of the 8th century. Length of the small belt-ends 4.7 cm. Nové Zámky. AÚ SAV

62. Large belt-end from plate 61. The crouching figure with the gesture of a suppliant is probably based on an oriental motif of an interceding spirit. Nové Zámky. AÚ SAV

63. Cast bronze belt-end with a figurative design of obscure significance (L 4 cm). Šebastovce. VM

64. Cast bronze belt loop with a figure of a gladiator, taken from a larger composition (2.5 × 2 cm). Hraničná nad Hornádom. VM

65. Cast bronze belt-end with an openwork figurative pattern (L 12.5 cm). The themes of the individual scenes are taken from the Hercules cycle. In the lower picture we see Hercules alone, with a club in his left hand and the skin of the Nemean lion in his right. In the center picture Hercules is killing the centaur Nessus; in the upper he is struggling with Hippolyte, the queen of the Amazons. The neck section of the belt-end depicts the wild boar killed by Hercules. The belt-end is a beautiful example of the revival of Hellenistic traditions. Dolné Dunajovice. MM

66. Cast bronze belt-end with the figure of a falconer. His costume is reminiscent of the Detva national costume of today (L 9 cm). Moravský Ján. Private Collection.

67. Bronze two-part clasp with a rose-pattern arrangement of colored stones (D 2.6 cm). Holiare. AÚ SAV

68. Bronze earrings with pendants of granulated wreaths and light blue beads (H 4 cm). Nové Zámky. AÚ SAV

69. Gold earrings with granulation and turquoise stones (H 4 cm). Želovce. AÚ SAV

70. Gilded bronze earrings with pendants of granulated wreaths and blue beads (H 4.2 cm). Holiare. AÚ SAV

71. Gold earrings with two-sided conical pendants with glass beads (H 4 cm). Želovce. AÚ SAV

72. A selection of gold earrings (H 2.2 cm, 3.4 cm, and 4 cm). Želovce. AÚ SAV

73. Bronze earring with pendant and five blue beads on the ring (H 3.1 cm). Holiare. AÚ SAV

74. Clay animal sculptures of ritual origin (L of the largest 15.5 cm). Mikulčice. NP

75. Examples of animal idols (L 5.5 and 7.5 cm). Mikulčice. NP

76. Examples of yellow pottery from Holiare (H 16.9 cm) and Nové Zámky (H 10 cm). AÚ SAV

77. Yellow pottery from graves. The bottle-like vessel (H 21.6 cm). The jug-like vessel with a broken handle (H 18 cm). Cup (H 10.5 cm). Nové Zámky. AÚ SAV

78. Pottery of the Danubian type, from graves (H 17 cm, 8.6 cm). Želovce. AÚ SAV

79. Openwork bronze ornament with a dualistic motif of a struggle between a griffin and a dragon (H 3 cm). Mikulčice. NP

80. Bronze ornament in the shape of a horse's head with a rich hammered semipalmette design (L 6 cm). Mikulčice. AÚ SAV

81. Cast bronze ornament in the shape of a boar's head with an engraved semipalmette design on a dotted background (L 7.2 cm). Three small bronze ornaments of identical shape (L 1.9 cm). Holiare. AÚ SAV

82. A selection of relics from the grave of a magnate. The gold plated escutcheon-shaped (H 3.4 cm), trapezium-shaped (H 3.2 cm), and tongue-shaped ornaments (H 2.9 and 3.4 cm) belong to the last stage of development of the cast bronze industry of the middle Danubian region. The key-shaped lateral loop (L 8.5 cm) and cross-shaped ornament (L 8.3 cm) with other fragments were part of a horse's harness. Length of the sword, 67.2 cm. Blatnica. MNM

83. Gilded bronze belt-end (L 9.2 cm), whose technology and ornamentation place it at the beginning of the Blatnica horizon. Žitavská Tôň. AÚ SAV

84. Gilded disc-shaped ornaments from the same set (D 2.3 cm). Žitavská Tôň. AÚ SAV

85. Cast bronze clasp with an openwork hinge plate (L 6 cm). Šaľa. AÚ SAV

86. Cast bronze openwork belt-end (L 8.8 cm). The stylized tree of life is an adaptation of an ancient Mediterranean symbol. Šaľa. AÚ SAV

87. Cast bronze rosette-shaped phalera (D 4 cm). Gajary. AÚ SNM

88. Hilt of a nobleman's sword (see plate 82) decorated with gilded bronze and inlaid with silver. The emphatically

geometric design combined with human masks points to Carolingian influence. Blatnica. MNM

89. Gilded cast bronze spurs whith semipalmette and mask decoration on the sectioned arms (L 11.6 cm and 12.1 cm). Mikulčice. NP

90. A set of gilded spurs with appurtenances. Strap end (L 2.3 cm) and buckle (L 5.1 cm) are decorated with the same semipalmette pattern. Mikulčice. NP

91. Bronze spurs inlaid with silver (L 11.3 cm) and appurtenances. Mikulčice. NP

92. Gilded bronze spurs with mask decoration, with appurtenances and gilded buttons. Mikulčice. NP

93. Gilded bronze belt-end decorated with a notched pattern (L 3.1 cm). Mikulčice. NP

94. Gilded bronze belt-end with a motif of stylized snakes entwined in a heart-shaped pattern (L 3.7 cm). Staré Město. MM

95. Gilded bronze clasp in the shape of birds (L 2.6 cm). Gilded bronze embossed belt-end (L 3 cm) and a gilded bronze clasp. Mikulčice. NP

96. Gilded bronze belt-end with a rich openwork plant pattern (L 6 cm). Mikulčice. NP

97. Oval gilded loop and gilded bronze belt-end with a stylized plant ornamentation using a notching technique. Staré Město. MM

98. Two gilded bronze cast belt-ends with openwork plant ornamentation (L 6 cm). Two gilded heart-shaped ornaments (H 3 cm). Two gilded ornaments with appendages (H 4.6 cm). Gilded bronze ornament made up of six masks (H 6.5 cm). Three gilded bronze triple-mask ornaments (H 3 cm). Žitavská Tôň. AÚ SNM

99. Detail of six-mask phalera made of heavily gilded bronze (plate 98). Žitavská Tôň. AÚ SNM

100. Gilded bronze ornament with a motif of schematized animal figures in typical insular style (L 3.7 cm). Hradec. M

101. Fragment of a gilded silver belt-end (L 5.2 cm). Confronting peacocks on either side of a stylized tree of life, in a medallion frame. The ribbons round the peacocks' necks point to Iranian influence. Mikulčice. NP

102. Obverse of a gilded silver belt-end with a wide, granulated edge and imitations of stones in the central field (L 5.9 cm). Mikulčice. NP

103. Flat reverse side of the belt-end (plate 102). The engraved figure of a suppliant with a gesture of adoration is thematically related to the motif of a mask and eyes on the "stones" of the obverse side. Mikulčice. NP

104. Gilded copper belt-end. The obverse has a plant motif framing a crouching frog (L 6.4 cm). Mikulčice. NP

105. Reverse side of belt-end (plate 104) with a very stylized figure of a man with the insignia of secular power and anointment. Mikulčice. NP

106. Parts of a horse's harness, made of iron, with a markedly divided relief decoration. Size of the cross-shaped ornament, 6.7 cm. Pobedim. AÚ SAV

107. Gilded silver earrings with a filigree crescent and grapelike pendant (H 3.1 cm). Holiare. AÚ SAV

108. Antler "salt cellar" decorated with an engraved geometrical pattern. Pobedim. AÚ SAV

109. Fragment of an antler hilt (L 9.6 cm) with a screw design. Mikulčice. NP
Bone whistle with an engraved geometrical pattern (L 9.6 cm). Staré Město. MM
Bone awl with a simple lattice design (L 10.3 cm). Nitra, Martinský vrch. AÚ SAV

110. Gilded silver reliquary in the likeness of a missal, richly decorated with granulation and filigree (L 3.9 cm). Mikulčice. NP

111. Gilded silver belt-end. Its wide, rounded frame is decorated with elements formed from chain filigree (L 3.9 cm). The central design is a mirror-picture of a branching pattern (L 6.7 cm). Mikulčice. NP

112. Obverse of belt-end (plate 111) with a stylized tree of life in a twisting frame. Mikulčice. NP

113. Belt-end of thin silver plate. The obverse has a dense network of interwoven vines and openwork strips with three symmetrically placed stones (L 7.2 cm). Mikulčice. NP

114. The reverse of the belt-end (plate 113) with a hammered and engraved figure of a suppliant man in a striking costume. Mikulčice. NP

115. Obverse of belt-end (plate 116) with a striking palmette design. Staré Město. OM Uherské Hradiště

116. Silver belt-end decorated with gold filigree and semiprecious stones (L 8 cm). Staré Město. OM Uherské Hradiště

117. Precious gold belt-end with an almandine (L 3.4 cm). Mikulčice, NP

118. Silver ornament with a carnelian, on which is engraved the figure of Eros with a cock (D 1.4 × 1.2 cm). Modrá. MM

119. Bead of millefiori glass. Staré Město. MM

120. Small belt-end with Greco-Roman gem. In addition to the head of Zeus and the eagle, there is also the portrait of the famous sculptor Feidias (L 2.4 cm). Mikulčice. NP

121. Gilded bronze cross with the figure of Christ the Suppliant, with the symbols of the sun and moon on the transverse arms and an omega below (H 4.3 cm, W 4.6 cm). Mikulčice. NP

122. Bronze two-part reliquary (H 6.8 cm, W 3.8 cm). Trnovec nad Váhom. AÚ SAV

123. Gilded bronze cross with masks (H 5.8 cm). Mikulčice. NP

124. Lead cross (H 2.8 cm). Mikulčice. NP

125. Necklace of glass beads with pendant lead crosses. Size of the crosses, 2 × 2.2 cm. Dolní Věstonice. MM

126. Cast silver cross with a crucified Christ (4.5 × 3.2 cm). Mikulčice. NP

127. Bronze reliquary with engraved figures of the three Marys (8.5 × 5.4 cm). Mača. AÚ SAV

128.—29. Double surfaced gold buttons decorated with filigree and latticework (3.3 × 3 cm). Mikulčice. NP

130. Lantern-shaped gold buttons with colored glass stones (H 2.5 cm). Mikulčice. NP

131. Silver ornament with the figure of a falconer (D 4 cm). Staré Město. MM

132.—33. Antler discs with designs of an animal fight and a kneeling archer in bas-relief (D 4.5 cm). Mikulčice. NP

134. Rosette and circular ornaments made from antlers (D 3.4 cm and 3.2 cm). Mikulčice. NP

135. Gilded bronze buttons of polygonal shape, from the 10th century (H 4.1 cm, D 3.6 cm). Nitra — Amphitheatre. AÚ SAV

136.—37. Set of buttons with a typical plant-palmette design. Staré Město. MM

138. Two-colored glass buttons (H 1.9 cm, D 1.6 cm). Staré Město. MM
Glass button in a silver plaited basket (H 3.1 cm). Břeclav, Pohansko. MM
Gold spherical button with granulated surface (H 2.8 cm, D 2.1 cm). Staré Město. MM

139. Gold and silver globular earrings with rich granulation (H 3.7 cm and 2.8 cm). Staré Město. MM

140. Gold earrings with two-sided globular pendant and six globules on the ring (H 4.5 cm). Silver globular earring with granulated wreath around the neck (H 5.5 cm). Staré Město. MM

141. Gold crescent-shaped earrings with globular pendants. Both the crescent and the globule are richly granulated (H 3.3 or 3.5 cm). Staré Město. MM

142. Silver and gilded earring with a column-shaped pendant finished at each end with a globule (H 3.8—4.5 cm). Staré Město. MM

143. Gold earring with an exceptional number of granulated globules (H 5.2). Mikulčice. NP

144. Silver basket-shaped earrings with filigree (H 4.3 cm) — the final phase of the Great Moravian traditions. Ducové. AÚ SAV

145. Gold basket-shaped earrings (H 5 cm). Staré Město. MM

146. Silver basket-shaped earring (H 5.7 cm). Trnovec nad Váhom. AÚ SAV

147. Silver earring with filigree baksets and a centrally set stone (H 5.2 cm). Staré Město. MM

148. Selection of gold crescent-shaped earrings with granulated

pendant. Upper and middle rows from Staré Město; below, Brno, Staré Zámky pri Líšni (H 2.5—3.8 cm). MM

149. Cast bronze crescent-shaped earring (H 4.2 cm). Nitra, Lupka. AÚ SAV

150.—51. Cast bronze earrings of a villein (H 4—4.2 cm). Nitra, Lupka. AÚ SAV

152. Three silver earrings with granulated lower arcs and two-sided grapelike pendants (H 2.5 cm). Staré Město. MM

153. Necklace of glass beads with a cast bronze lunar pendant (W of the pendant 4 cm). Dolní Věstonice. MM

154. Necklace of millefiori beads with a lunar pendant (W of the pendant 4.4 cm). Staré Město

155. Necklace with paste beads and a bronze lunar pendant (W of the pendant 4 cm). Nitra, Lupka. AÚ SAV

156. Cast bronze lunar pendant with its points turned inward (W 3 cm). Nitra, Lupka. AÚ SAV

157. Silver lunar pendant with fine granulation on its geometrically divided surface (W 6.6. cm). Staré Město. MM

158. Gold lunar pendant, its edge decorated with chain filigree and center with granulated triangles and rhombuses (W 2.6 cm). Mikulčice. NP

159. Pendant from the necklace (plate 155). Nitra, Lupka. AÚ SAV

160. Millefiori beads. Staré Město. MM

161. Necklace of blown glass, barrel-shaped beads. Staré Město. MM

162. Silver ring with a stone and granulation (D 3 cm, D of the mounting 2.2 cm). Mikulčice. NP

163. Silver ring with granulation, filigree, and blue stones. Mikulčice. NP

164. Gilded silver ring with granulation (D 1.8 cm). Silver cylinder-shaped reliquary decorated with filigree (D 4.2 cm). Staré Město. MM

165. Ritual twin vessel of smooth clay (H 9 cm). Staré Město. MM

166. Disc-shaped gilded bronze clasp (D 4.8 cm). Staré Město. MM

167. Silver earring with chain pendant and finely granulated zoomorphic figure on the lower arc of the ring. Stará Kouřim. MM

168. Silver earrings with chain pendants and a motif of a crescent on one, a mitre on the other lower arc of the ring (H 15.4 cm and 17 cm). Stará Kouřim. NM

169. Bronze and silvered semicircular cylindrical amulets decorated with filigree and granulation. Stará Kouřim. NM

170. Spherical granulated "pearl" and silver buttons with a raised design. Stará Kouřim. NM

171. Gold earrings with two-sided cornlike pendants. Stará Kouřim. NM

172. Necklace with glass beads covered with gold foil, amethyst beads, and silver filigree baskets — a clear example of the dying out of Great Moravian traditions in the early feudal Hungarian kingdom. Ducové. AÚ SAV

173. Gilded silver belt-end with loops. Kolín. NM

174. Silver ornaments of the Carolingian type inset with niello, from the straps holding a sword. Kolín. NM

175. Gold chain with a Greco-Roman gem in an oval medallion. Želénky. NM

176. Gold chain with a gold medallion. Želénky. NM

177.—78. Obverse and reverse of a gilded ornament with a picture of a falcon or an eagle attacking a deer. Želénky. NM

179. Foundations of a church. Pohansko, Břeclav

180. Foundations of the triple-aisle basilica. Mikulčice

181. Foundations of a mausoleum. Mikulčice

182. Foundations of a complex of church buildings. Sady, Uherské Hradiště

183. Foundations of a rotunda with two apses. Mikulčice

184. Foundations of a church with a square apse and supporting pillars. Mikulčice

185. Foundations of residential buildings on a magnate's estate. Pohansko, Břeclav

186. Foundations of a rotunda. Ducové, Moravany

Åberg, Nils: *Die Goten und Langobarden in Italien.* Uppsala — Leipzig 1923.

Arbman, Holger: *Schweden und das Karolingische Reich.* Stockholm 1937.

Arbman, Holger: "Blatnica und Vaage." *Památky archeologické* 53, 1962, pp. 331—338.

Bank, Alica Vladimirovna: *Vizantijskoe iskusstvo v sobranijach Sovetskogo Sojuza.* Leningrad 1966.

Beckwith, John: *Coptic Sculpture.* London 1963.

Beckwith, John: *Early Medieval Art.* London 1964.

Benda, Klement: "Contribution à l'étude du style des parures de la Grande Moravie." *Byzantinoslavica* 22, 1961, pp. 55—64.

Benda, Klement: "Pozdně avarské nákončí z hrobu 22 v Modré u Velehradu." *Památky archeologické* 53, 1962, pp. 339—346.

Benda, Klement: "Stříbrný terč se sokolníkem ze Starého Města u Uherského Hradiště." *Památky archeologické* 54, 1963, pp. 41—66.

Benda, Klement: "Karolinská zložka blatnického nálezu." *Slovenská archeológia* 11, 1963, pp. 199—222.

Benda, Klement: *Das großmährische Kunsthandwerk, Großmähren-Slawenreich zwischen Byzantinern und Franken.* Ausstellungskatalog 1 des Römisch-Germanischen Zentralmuseums, Mainz — Bonn 1966, pp. 69.

Benda, Klement: *Mittelalterlicher Schmuck* (Slawische Funde aus tschechoslowakischen Sammlungen und Leningrader Ermitage). Praha 1966.

Bialeková, Darina: "Žltá keramika z pohrebísk obdobia avarskej ríše v Karpatskej kotline." *Slovenská archeológia* 15, 1967, pp. 5—76.

Bialeková, Darina: "Výskum slovanského hradiska v Pobedime r. 1964." *Archeologické rozhledy* 17, 1965, pp. 516, 530—538.

Bialeková, Darina: "Výskum slovanského hradiska v Pobedime, okr. Trenčín." *Archeologické rozhledy* 24, 1972, pp. 121—129.

Bialeková, Darina — Pieta, Karol: "Zisťovací výskum v Hradci, okres Prievidza." *Slovenská archeológia* 12, 1964, pp. 447 n.

Böhm, Jaroslav: "Deux églises datant de l'Empire de la Grande-Moravie découvertes en Tchécoslovaquie." *Byzantinoslavica* 11, 1950, pp. 207—222.

Böhm, Jaroslav: "Dva kostely z doby říše Velkomoravské." *Památky archeologické* 46, 1955, pp. 358—372.

Böhm, Jaroslav: "K rozboru kostela v Modré u Velehradu." *Acta Universitatis Carolinae — Philosophica et Historica* 3, 1960, pp. 273—284.

Bréhier, Louis: *La sculpture et les arts mineurs — Histoire de l'art byzantin.* Paris 1936.

Budinský-Krička, Vojtech: "Pohrebisko z doby avarskej v Žitavskej Tôni na Slovensku." *Slovenská archeológia* 4, 1956, pp. 5—131.

Budinský-Krička, Vojtech: "Slovanské mohyly v Skalici." *Archaeologica Slovaca — Fontes 2,* Bratislava 1959.

Byvanck, A. W.: "Les origines de l'art copt." *Orientalia neerlandica,* London 1948, pp. 111—115.

Capelle, Torsten: "Karolingischer Schmuck in der Tschechoslowakei." *Slovenská archeológia* 16, 1968, pp. 229—224.

Cibulka, Josef: "Zur Frühgeschichte der Architektur in Mähren (800—900)." *Festschrift Karl M. Swoboda zum 28. Januar 1959,* Köln — Graz 1959, pp. 55—74.

Cibulka, Josef: "Großmährische Kirchenbauten" Sancti Cyrillus et Methodius — Leben und Wirken, Praha 1963, pp. 49—117.

164 Cibulka, Josef: *Velkomoravský kostel v Modré u Velehradu a začátky křesťanství na Moravě.* Praha 1958.

Čilinská, Zlata: "Nové nálezy falér zo slovansko-avarských pohrebísk na Slovensku." *Slovenská archeológia* 9, 1961, pp. 325—346.

Čilinská, Zlata: "Slovansko-avarské pohrebisko v Žitavskej Tôni." *Slovenská archeológia* 11, 1963, pp. 87—120.

Čilinská, Zlata: "Slawisch-awarisches Gräberfeld in Nové Zámky." *Archaeologica Slovaca — Fontes,* Bratislava 1966.

Čilinská, Zlata: *Frühmittelalterliches Gräberfeld in Želovce.* Bratislava 1971.

Ćorović-Ljubinković, Mirjana: "Der Zusammenhang des Schmuckes des Nitra-Gebietes und Nordserbiens in IX. Jahrhundert." *Slovenská archeológia* 18, 1970, pp. 113—117.

Dalton, O. M.: *Byzantin Art and Archaeology.* Oxford 1911.

Dekan, Ján: "Les motifs figuraux humains sur les bronzes moulés de la zone danubienne centrale à l'époque précédent l'émpire de la Grande Moravie." *Studia Historica Slovaca* 2, 1964.

Dekan, Ján: "O genéze výtvarného prejavu Veľkej Moravy." *Výtvarný život* 8, 1963, pp. 283—290.

Dekan, Ján: "Die Beziehungen unserer Länder mit dem Spätantiken und byzantinischen Gebiet in der Zeit vor Cyrill und Method." Das Großmährische Reich. Praha 1966, pp. 89—102.

Dekan, Ján: "Herkunft und Ethnizität der gegossenen Bronzeindustrie des VIII. Jahrhunderts." *Slovenská archeológia* 20, 1972.

Denkstein, Vladimír: "K ikonografii mikulčického nákončí." *Památky archeologické* 52, 1961, pp. 650 n.

Diehl, Charles: *Manuel d'art byzantin.* Paris 1925.

Dostál, Bořivoj: *Slovanská pohřebiště ze střední doby hradištní na Moravě,* Praha 1966.

Dostál, Bořivoj: "Das Vordringen der großmährischen materiellen Kultur in die Nachbarländer." *Magna Moravia,* Praha 1965, pp. 361—416.

Eisner, Jan: "Dvě přilby typu baldenheimského z Poiplí." *Historica Slovaca* 3—4, 1945—46.

Eisner, Jan: "K dějinám našeho hradištního šperku." *Časopis Národního musea* 1947.

Eisner, Jan: *Devínska Nová Ves.* Bratislava 1952.

Erdélyi, István: *Die Kunst der Awaren.* Budapest 1966.

Fettich, Nándor: "Die Tierkampfszene in der Nomadenkunst." Recueil d'études dédiées á la mémoire de N. P. Kondakov. Praha 1926, pp. 81—92.

Fettich, Nándor: "Bronzeguß und Nomadenkunst." *Seminarium Kondakovianum,* Prague 1929, pp. 55—81.

Fettich, Nándor: "Die Metallkunst der landnehmenden Ungarn." *Acta Archeologica Hungarica* 21, 1937.

Fettich, Nándor: *Archäologische Studien zur Geschichte der späthunnischen Metallkunst.* Budapest 1951.

Gervers-Molnár, V.: *A középkori Magyarország rotundái.* (Művészettörténeti füzetek 4), Budapest 1972.

Ghirshman, R.: *Iran. Parther und Sasseniden.* München 1962.

Goldschmidt, Adolph: *Die Elfenbeinskulpturen aus der Zeit der karolingischen und sächsischen Kaiser.* Berlin 1914.

Grube, Ernst: *Islamské umenie.* Pallas, Bratislava 1973.

Hampel, József: *Alterthümer des frühen Mittelalters in Ungarn* 1.—3. Braunschweig 1905.

Haseloff, Günther: *Der Tassilo Kelch.* 1952.

Havlík, Lubomír: *Velká Morava a středoevropští Slované.* Praha 1964.

Henry, F.: *Irish Art in the Early Christian Period.* 1965.

Hrubý, Vilém: *Staré Město — Velkomoravské pohřebiště "Na valách".* Praha 1955.

Hrubý, Vilém: *Staré Město — Velkomoravský Velehrad.* Praha 1965.

Hrubý, Vilém: "Keramika antických tvarů v době velkomoravské." *Časopis Moravského Musea* 50, 1965, pp. 37—62.

Hrubý, Vilém — Hochmanová, V. — Pavelčík, J.: "Kostel a pohřebiště z doby velkomoravské na Modré u Velehradu." *Časopis Moravského Musea* 40, 1955, pp. 42—126.

Chropovský, Bohuslav: "Slovanské pohrebisko v Nitre na Lupke." *Slovenská archeológia* 10, 1962, pp. 175—240.

Chropovský, Bohuslav: "The Situation of Nitra in the Light of Archaeological Finds." *Historica* 8, 1964, pp. 5—33.

Chropovský, Bohuslav: *Slovensko na úsvite dejín.* Bratislava 1970.

Kalousek, František: *Břeclav-Pohansko, Velkomoravské pohřebiště u kostela.* Brno 1971.

Karger, Michail Konstantinovič: *Drevnij Kijev 1.* Moskva—Leningrad 1958.

Kidson, Peter: *Stredoveké umenie.* Pallas, Bratislava 1974.

Klanica, Zdeněk: "Velkomoravský gombík." *Archeologické rozhledy* 22, 1970, pp. 426 n.

Klanica, Zdeněk: "Předvelkomoravské pohřebiště v Dolních Dunajovicích. Příspěvek k otázce vzájemných vztahů Slovanů a Avarů v Podunají." *Studie Archeologického ústavu Československé akademie věd v Brně* 1, 1972.

Kostka, Jiří: "Monumentálna architektúra Veľkomoravskej ríše." *Výtvarný život* 8, 1963, pp. 291—303.

Korzuchina, Gali Fedorovna: *Russkie klady 9—12 vv.* Moskva—Leningrad 1954.

Kraskovská, Ľudmila: "Skvosty z doby hradištnej na Slovensku." *Slavia Antiqua* 1, Poznań 1948.

Kraskovská, Ľudmila: "Pohrebisko v Bernolákove." *Slovenská archeológia* 10, 1962, pp. 425—476.

Kraskovská, Ľudmila: *Slovansko-avarské pohrebisko pri Záhorskej Bystrici.* Bratislava 1972.

Kotrba, Viktor: "Církevní stavby Velké Moravy." *Umění* 12, 1964, pp. 325—361.

Lassus, Jean: *Ranokresťanské a byzantské umenie.* Pallas, Bratislava 1971.

László, Gyula: *Études archeologiques sur l'histoire de la société des Avars.* Budapest 1955.

László, Gyula: *Steppenvölker und Germanen (Kunst der Völkerwanderungszeit).* Wien—München 1970.

Mavrodinov, Nicolas: *Le trésor protobulgare de Nagyszentmiklós.* Budapest 1943.

Merhautová-Livorová, Anežka: "Einfache mitteleuropäische Rundkirchen — Ihr Ursprung, Zweck und ihre Bedeutung." *Rozpravy Československé akademie věd* 1970.

Mitscha-Märheim, Herbert: *Dunkler Jahrhunderte goldene Spuren.* Wien 1963.

Niederle, Lubomír: *Příspěvky k vývoji byzantských šperků ze IV.—X. století.* Praha 1930.

Pauliny, Eugen: *Slovesnosť a kultúrny jazyk Veľkej Moravy.* Bratislava 1964.

Pošmourný, Josef: "Budownictwo murowane Słowian wielkomorawskich." *Kwartalnik historii kultury materialnej* 17, 1969, pp. 633—678.

Pošmourný, Josef: "Provenience stavebního umění velkomoravských Slovanů." *Zborník filozofickej fakulty Univerzity Komenského — Musaica* 11, 1971, pp. 41—60.

Poulík, Josef: "Záhadná mohyla Žuráň," *Archeologické rozhledy* 1, 1949.

Poulík, Josef: *Staroslovanská Morava.* Praha 1948.

Poulík, Josef: *Jižní Morava, země dávných Slovanů.* Brno 1948—1950.

Poulík, Josef: "Výsledky výzkumu na velkomoravském hradišti ‚Valy' u Mikulčic." *Památky archeologické 48,* 1957, pp. 241—374.

Poulík, Josef: "Nález kostela z doby velkomoravské v trati ‚Špitálky' ve Starém Městě." *Památky archeologické 46,* 1955.

Poulík, Josef: *Dvě velkomoravské rotundy v Mikulčicích.* Praha 1963.

Poulík, Josef: *Pevnost v lužním lese.* Praha 1967.

Poulík, Josef: "Beziehungen Großmährens zu den europäischen Kulturgebieten." *Jahrbuch für Landeskunde von Niederösterreich, Neue Folge 38* (1968—69). Wien 1970, pp. 124—144.

Poulík, Josef: *Mikulčice. Sídlo a pevnost knížat velkomoravských.* Praha 1975.

Ratkoš, Peter: "Veľkomoravské obdobie v slovenských dejinách." *Historický časopis* 6, 1958, pp. 3—31.

Ratkoš, Peter: *Pramene k dejinám Veľkej Moravy.* II. vydanie, Bratislava 1968.

Richter, Václav: "Die Anfänge der großmährischen Architektur." *Magna Moravia*, Praha 1965, pp. 121—360.

Ross, C. Marvin: *Catalogue of the Byzantine and early Medieval Antiquities in the Dumbarton Oaks Collection 2*. Washington 1965.

Rybakov, Boris Alexandrovič: *Remeslo drevnej Rusi*. Moskva—Leningrad 1948.

Sarre, Friedrich: *Die Kunst des alten Persien*. Berlin 1922.

Sós-Cs., Ágnes: *Bemerkungen zur Problematik des Kirchenbaus des 9. Jahrhunderts in Transdanubien*. (Liber Josepho Kostrzewski octogenario a veneratoribus dedicatus), Wrocław—Warszawa—Kraków 1968.

Sós-Cs., Ágnes: *Die Ausgrabungen Géza Fehérs in Zalavár*. Budapest 1963.

Strzygowski, Józef: *Die altslawische Kunst*. Augsburg 1929.

Strzygowski, Józef: *Iran und Völkerwanderung*. Leipzig 1917.

Svoboda, Bedřich: "Poklad byzantského kovotepca v Zemianském Vrbovku." *Památky archeologické* 44, 1953, pp. 33—93.

Svoboda, Bedřich: "Zum Problem antiker Traditionen in der ältesten slawischen Kultur." *Origines et débuts des Slaves* 6, 1966, pp. 87—114.

Szőke, Béla: "Über die Beziehungen Moraviens zu dem Donaugebiet in der Spätawarenzeit." *Studia Slavica* 6, 1960, pp. 75—112.

Šolle, Miloš: "Čechy v době rozkvětu velkomoravských center." *Slovenská archeológia* 18—1, 1970, pp. 129—136.

Šolle, Miloš: "Knížecí pohřebiště ve Staré Kouřimi." *Památky archeologické* 50, 1959, pp. 353—506.

Štefanovičová, Tatiana — Fiala, Andrej: "Veľkomoravská bazilika, kostol sv. Salvátora a pohrebisko na Bratislavskom hrade." *Zborník Filozofickej fakulty Univerzity Komenského — Historica* 18, 1967, pp. 151—216.

Talbot Rice, David: *Byzantské umenie*. Tatran, Bratislava 1968.

Talbot Rice, Tamara: *Ancient Arts of Central Asia*. London 1965.

Točík, Anton: "Pohrebisko a sídlisko z doby avarskej ríše v Prši." *Slovenská archeológia* 11, 1963, pp. 121—198.

Točík, Anton: *Slawisch-awarisches Gräberfeld in Holiare*. Bratislava 1968.

Točík, Anton: *Slawisch-awarisches Gräberfeld in Štúrovo*. Bratislava 1968.

Turek, Rudolf: *Čechy na úsvitě dějin*. Praha 1963.

Turek, Rudolf: "K otázce vlivů a tradic velkomoravské architektury v Čechách." *Slovenská archeológia* 18, 1970, pp. 153—158.

Turek, Rudolf: "K problému stop cyrilometodějské misie ve hmotné kultuře Velké Moravy." *Slavia* 38, 1969, pp. 616—626.

Vavřínek, Vladimír: *Církevní misie v dějinách Velké Moravy*. Praha 1963.

Vavřínek, Vladimír: "Die Christianisierung und Kirchenorganisation Großmährens." *Historica* 7, 1963, pp. 5—56.

Vavřínek, Vladimír: "Study of the Church Architecture from the Period of the Great Moravian Empire." *Byzantinoslavica* 25, 1964, pp. 288—301.

Venedikov, Ivan: *Alte Schätze Bulgarien*. Sofia 1965.

Volbach, Wolfgang Fritz: *Elfenbeinskulpturen der Spätantike und des frühen Mittelalters*. Mainz 1952.

Werner, Joachim: "Slawische Bügelfibeln des 7. Jahrhunderts." *Reinecke Festschrift,* Mainz 1950, pp. 150—172.

Werner, Joachim: "Neues zur Frage der slawischen Bügelfibeln aus südosteuropäischen Ländern." *Germania* 38, 1960.

Werner, Joachim: "Zur Verbreitung frühgeschichtlicher Metallarbeiten." *Antikvarist Arkiv* 38, 1970, pp. 65—81.

Wessel, Klaus: *Koptische Kunst. Die Spätantike in Ägypten.* Recklingshausen 1963.

Wulf, Oskar: *Altchristliche und Byzantinische Kunst* 1—2. Berlin 1913—1918.

Almanach Veľká Morava. Brno 1965.

Istorija iskusstva narodov SSSR — 2. *Iskusstvo IV—XII vekov.* Moskva 1973.

Magna Moravia. Sborník k 1100. výročí příchodu byzantské mise na Moravu, Praha 1965.

Veľká Morava. Tisícročná tradícia štátu a kultúry. Praha 1963.